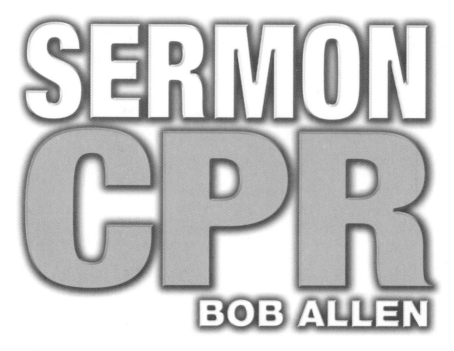

SERMON CPR

BOB ALLEN

Resuscitating Your Preaching Style

D1292281

Beacon Hill Press of Kansas City
Kansas City, Missouri

ISBN 083-412-2111

Printed in the
United States of America

Cover Design: Paul Franitza

All Scripture quotations not otherwise designated are from the King James Version. Permission to quote from the following copyrighted versions of the Scriptures is acknowledged with appreciation:

The *New American Standard Bible*® (NASB®), © copyright The Lockman Foundation 1960, 1962, 1963, 1968, 1971, 1973, 1975, 1977, 1995.

The *Holy Bible, New International Version*® (NIV®). Copyright © 1973, 1978, 1984 by International Bible Society. Used by permission of Zondervan Publishing House. All rights reserved.

The *New King James Version* (NKJV). Copyright © 1979, 1980, 1982 Thomas Nelson, Inc.

The *New Revised Standard Version* (NRSV) of the Bible, copyright 1989 by the Division of Christian Education of the National Council of the Churches of Christ in the USA. Used by permission. All rights reserved.

Library of Congress Cataloging-in-Publication Data

Allen, Bob, 1946 Nov. 27-
  Sermon CPR : resuscitating your preaching style / Bob Allen.
    p. cm.
  Includes bibliographical references.
  ISBN 0-8341-2211-1 (pbk.)
 1. Preaching. 2. Public speaking—Religious aspects—Christianity. I. Title.
  BV4211.3.A424 2005
  251—dc22
                                        2005002355

10 9 8 7 6 5 4 3 2 1

To my parents,
Dr. and Mrs. Arthur Allen
and my wife's parents,
Dr. and Mrs. Arthur Odens,
whose combined years of ministry
have provided consistent models of exemplary
Christian character and service

Contents

Acknowledgments

Thanks to the dedicated servants at Beacon Hill Press of Kansas City, particularly Richard E. Buckner, who has worked with me on the editing and preparation of this manuscript.

Thanks also to the four churches that have helped me improve skills in preaching, and to the students at Liberty University, Pillsbury Baptist Bible College, and Baptist Bible College of Pennsylvania, who have allowed me to have a part in their preparation for ministry.

1
Satellite Channel Listeners

■ The auditorium of First Church of Central City, familiar territory to Dr. Prescott, often figured prominently in his dreams. On this particular night the auditorium had been transformed into an ultramodern communications center for the 21st century. Pews had given way to padded theater seats, each one equipped with its own monitor and earphones so no one would miss even one sound or nuance of the sermon he had so carefully prepared.

Dr. Prescott had been preaching for more than 30 years, and though he suspected that certain individuals within his congregation tuned him out from week to week, he had never imagined anything like the sight that greeted him in his dream.

As he preached, his parishioners openly flaunted their remote controls, surfing the seemingly endless satellite channels on the individual television units mounted on the seats in front of them. Young Brad Esterson watched football on ESPN, listening to a team of commentators who rattled off an endless supply of colorful trivia about the players on both teams. That didn't surprise Dr. Prescott; Brad thought about little else but football all week, so why should it be different on Sunday?

Mrs. Patterson did surprise him though. Her facial expression and frequent note taking had always convinced him she listened closely. But there she was watching a different service altogether, one from a large church in the south with a young, eloquent minister who had always impressed Dr. Prescott as a cross between Dr. Phil and David Letterman.

Some of the young girls viewed music videos with their ever-changing sounds and images, while a few of the men created their own videos by zapping rapidly through the available channels as if trying to watch all of the pictures at the same time.

The chaotic scene morphed, as dreams have a tendency to do, into a wall of television screens. Dr. Prescott could see instantly what every person in the auditorium was watching. Not even his wife was watching his channel; she had tuned in the latest episode of one of those home-improvement programs.

But someone had to be watching because he was right there on the wall of screens along with everyone else—competing. That's what it was. He was competing for the attention of his own listeners with every other voice they had heard during the week.

His tonal quality was compared to that of news anchors like Tom Brokaw. His gestures and movements were contrasted to those of sports-casters like Terry Bradshaw. His forcefulness and persuasiveness competed with that of Bill O'Reilly. It wasn't fair.

To his great disappointment, that dream proved to be one of the few Dr. Prescott remembered after waking up. It haunted him for weeks. Every time he stepped into the pulpit, he found himself trying to peer into the minds of his listeners, seeking to determine whether they were really paying attention.

It wasn't the content of his sermons that worried him. Thirty years of diligent Bible study securely rooted in his college and seminary training in Greek and Hebrew convinced him he had a message his people needed to hear. He had no doubt he was faithfully communicating the Word of God.

What worried him was his dream—the competition. Hollywood actors took classes from private tutors on how to use their voices for the greatest emotional impact. Politicians hired coaches who trained them in everything from facial expression to the correct pronunciation of the names of foreign leaders.

Dr. Prescott's entire preparation in the area of speech delivery had been a required semester course his freshman year in college, almost 35 years before. The years of ministry since then had passed so quickly that there had been little time for a refresher course. Until the nightmare had surfaced, he had to admit the subject of his pulpit delivery had seldom even occurred to him. The church was full every Sunday. People must be listening.

But now he wondered. And comments overheard during his waking hours started to intermingle with his dream. He remembered his aging mother complaining about a speaker at a conference she attended.

"When he shouted, I had to turn my hearing aid down," she said. "When he whispered, I couldn't hear him even if I turned it way up. Finally, I just turned off the hearing aid and tried to read his lips."

On another occasion a young couple who had visited the church shared their dilemma. The husband had been raised in church and liked sermons to follow a logical outline. The wife was a great reader and liked stories. She didn't really care if the sermon proceeded logically as long as the story spoke to her heart. The unspoken message that Dr. Prescott heard was that his style of preaching appealed to people's minds but missed their hearts.

Then, one night after church, he walked past a nearly empty classroom from which uncontrolled laughter echoed. Without being observed, he watched as a junior high boy provided a hilarious rendition of his own preaching. He had the stock phrases down pat. "Let me direct your attention to the valuable nuggets mined from today's treasure trove of Scripture." The stance behind the pulpit remained formal, broken only by what had to be an overexaggerated gesture. The boy would take two steps backward, hitch up his pants, and then move toward the pulpit as if it were under attack. That was the action that brought gales of laughter from the other boys in the room.

Without making his presence known, Dr. Prescott walked down the hallway to his study, determined to discover the truth about his preaching. He wasn't about to change his message—but he had to know if his methods were really communicating that message. He had to know if the mental remote controls of his weekly audience were in tune with what he was trying to say.

2
Listening to Your Own Preaching

■ If the experience of Dr. Prescott sounded familiar to you, consider this scenario. It is one o'clock in the afternoon on Sunday. The service is over, and you are starting to unwind. Your mind replays the preaching event, dwelling joyously on certain aspects of the sermon and wondering how other elements could have been improved. Like Dr. Prescott, you wonder whether your listeners were tuned in to what you were saying. But there is little time for reflection. That sermon has been delivered.

So what can you do? The sermon is no longer yours. You have delivered it, set it free, released it. Plus there is so little time for analysis because another sermon must soon take its place. Is there some way to improve your next sermon? If not, how about the one after that? Perhaps the best way to look for answers is to take a fresh look at preaching in general.

The act of preaching involves two distinct components. The first one, the preparation that takes place in the study, remains unseen, although its results are quite evident in the outline and word choice. The second component, by contrast, is performed in full view of the listening audience. It involves the delivery of the sermon with all of its oral, visual, and stylistic parts. That is the component the listeners identify as the sermon.

Ironically, the integral part of preaching most visible to a congregation often consumes little of the preacher's attention during the preparation of the sermon. Instead, the focus is on the content of the message—on the story. That leaves little time to think about delivery.

On top of this, the majority of books written about homiletics concentrate on the first component of preaching. They emphasize research and are very valuable during the week when preparing sermons but not on Sunday when delivering them. Some books include a brief section on delivery, but their focus is definitely on study and preparation. This is also the case with most college and seminary homiletics classes, which focus on the process of preparation rather than delivery. According to Jerry Vines' *A Guide to Effective Sermon Delivery*, "Little training is provided in how to deliver the message utilizing the various techniques of effective speech communication."[1] Both the books and classes stress that content must precede delivery, that what we say is more important than how we say it, and that is certainly true. Fluency of speech combined with emptiness of the head will never meet the needs of any except those who listen with "itching ears" (2 Tim. 4:3).

At the same time, fidelity to content must not overlook the development of a sermon's delivery. The preacher who develops narrative messages will need to be aware of how he or she meets the physical and oral demands of the narrative preaching style. The communicator who prefers expository or topical preaching must likewise give attention to delivery because he or she will be competing against the many voices of today's media culture.

Once the preacher learns to dive into the depths of Scripture and discover pearls, the concern for how those pearls are displayed must grow in importance. "Sermons do not come into the world as outlines or manuscripts," wrote Haddon Robinson in *Biblical Preaching*. "They live only when preached. A sermon ineptly delivered arrives stillborn."[2]

The Book of Proverbs provides a striking image of the relationship between content and delivery: "A word fitly spoken is like apples of gold in a setting of silver" (25:11, NRSV). If the apples represent a message's content, the "silver setting" represents its delivery. No one would take a solid gold apple and display it in a plastic pail full of dirt. The method of display reflects its value and should enhance its beauty.

Inattention to delivery can devalue carefully prepared content. "Indeed it is possible for a week's effort on sermon preparation to be wasted by fifteen minutes' poor delivery,"[3] D. W. Cleverly Ford wrote in *The Ministry of the Word*. The time, skill, and energy expended in understanding the text and shaping the sermon's structure to complement it will be of little value if the delivery obscures the message. *Preaching Is Dialogue*, by Henry Eggold, summarizes the subject in these words, "The moment of delivery is the time of success or failure in preaching."[4]

Good delivery does matter. When you know that the content of the story has been successfully captured in the study during the week, it is discouraging to see boredom on the faces of listeners. That boredom may well be due to a late Saturday night, but it may also be due to the poor delivery of the speaker. Haddon Robinson reminds us that "every empirical study of delivery and its effect on the outcome of a speech or sermon arrives at an identical conclusion: delivery matters a great deal."[5] Nonverbal communication can contradict the verbal message. Body language can distract. Lack of vocal variety can so alienate a listener as to obscure the intended communication. Word choice can frustrate audiences who fail to understand the approach used by the speaker. All of these, along with the methods of organization, can detract from the communication of the story listeners so desperately need to hear.

What we must do is seek to hone delivery skills to where they will provide a frame for the Word of God that will enhance the story and make it both palatable and memorable for listeners. We want them to hear the story, and that means we need to be diligent in how it is told.

Some of the preachers who neglect the practice and improvement of delivery skills repeat idiosyncratic behaviors that hinder communication. They develop sloppy verbal habits, such as excessively rapid speech, that prevent listeners from even hearing much of what is said. They spend minimal time on word choice, electing instead to use whatever words come to mind at the moment of extemporaneous delivery. To the credit of their congregations, people learn to adjust to such inadequacies. But they should not be required to make that adjustment. How much better it would be if the speaker would adjust to the communication needs of the listeners. Hours in the study are extremely important, but "the real dilemma is to get God's message, which exists in the mind of the preacher, to the hearer with the greatest amount of understanding and the least amount of distortion."[6]

John Broadus warns of the danger of not giving enough attention to how a message is presented, while at the same time providing some excellent advice:

> The difference between skill and the lack of it in speaking is almost as great as in handling tools, those for example, of the carpenter or the blacksmith. And while no real skill can be acquired without practice—according to the true saying, "the only way to learn to preach is to preach,"—yet mere practice will never bring the highest skill; it must be heedful, thoughtful practice, with close observation

of others and sharp watching of ourselves, and controlled good sense and good taste."[7]

The ideal arrangement for any preacher would be to have in the congregation a mentor who could regularly offer incisive, positive feedback about his or her preaching. Clearly, that would require a special relationship of trust and expertise not available in most situations. In churches with a pastoral team, such a mentorship might be possible provided the team members are not overloaded with other work. A senior pastor with only a youth pastor on staff will usually discover that his or her associate is more than sufficiently occupied.

Enrolling in continuing education classes or seminars on preaching is another option. This can be extremely beneficial, although such classes and seminars usually consist of group instruction rather than personalized mentorship. The greatest improvement in delivery skill usually takes place when a preacher receives detailed comments about his or her own strengths and weaknesses. He or she needs an analysis with accompanying exercises to correct deficiencies and reinforce strengths. Unless a preacher makes a deliberate choice to perform a self-evaluation, he or she probably will not get the help needed.

One reason it is hard to get help from others is something almost all of us have to admit—we do not accept criticism easily, even from someone as close as a spouse. It is a relief to learn from Robert Delnay, in his book *Fire in Your Pulpit*, that this is not just a problem for preachers. "After all, parents are sensitive about their children, writers about their articles, and surgeons about their surgeries. However, while parents learn to discipline, while writers revise their work, and while surgeons do autopsies, we may wonder how many preachers critique their own preaching."[8]

A preacher who has studied diligently and believes he or she possesses a good understanding of a text often resents the suggestion that the presentation of those truths could actually be obscuring the message. Yet that same person, when asked, can recognize inadequacies in the delivery of others. The best way for a preacher to improve is to learn to listen to his or her sermons the way others do.

The first step in acquiring better delivery skills is the recognition on the part of the preacher that improvement is needed. As long as a person is satisfied with his or her vocal, physical, and stylistic presentation, he or she will not seek help. C. Jeff Woods put it this way, "All pastors are capable of improving their ministry competencies. Most pastors say that they desire regular improvement. Secretly tucked away in the concept of improvement, however, is the C Word. That's right—CHANGE! And that's the problem."[9] Preachers are naturally motivated to improve their understanding of the Word, but they often resist the idea that they need to change their pulpit style.

An unwillingness to change can erect major communication barriers. Just look at how the congregation responds in this description by Stevenson and Diehl:

> In the realm of ideas the lightning flashed, the thunder roared, the heavens opened as the voice of God rolled forth, but not more than a man here and there throughout the congregation had any awareness of what was going on. The rest of the people just sat and endured it. They heard no voice of God: they heard a man mumbling, and—mentally at least—they fell asleep.[10]

People who fall asleep when we preach may say they lost sleep working late the night before. Yet the suspicion remains that their inattention is really due to our weak communication skills. Richard Balge and Joel Gerlach in *Preach the Gospel* remind us that "some sermons a person can listen to; some he can't listen to; and some he can't help listening to. Probably more than any other single factor, delivery makes the difference."[11] The preacher who has a message from God, who is convinced that the "story" must be heard, will desire to preach sermons people "can't help listening to."

Preachers offer a variety of excuses for not giving greater attention to improving their pulpit delivery. Some argue that developing better oral and body language skills produces artificiality. They have heard a preacher who tried to imitate someone else, perhaps a well-known evangelist, and they equate that mistake with what it takes to become a more effective speaker. The interest of this book is in developing a preacher's own personal style. There is value in listening to others, but not for the purpose of sounding like them. D. W. Ford says, "The truth, however, is that artificiality indicates that the work on the delivery has been unthorough. A preacher who is not himself in the pulpit has a great deal to learn."[12]

It is certainly possible to develop personal delivery skills without becoming artificial. David Larsen explains that "delivery must basically come from our own natures."[13] Poor delivery will distort an audience's perception of the emotions and inner nature of the preacher just as quickly as a perceived artificiality. To become effective tellers of the story, we must eliminate anything that distracts from the communication process.

The best method of personal improvement you will ever discover is self-evaluation. Comparisons with other preachers will either discourage or cause undue self-congratulation. Although the awareness of competing voices may impel you to seek improvement, comparison with yourself is the best way to succeed. "The key to enhancing substantive and lasting improvement in any group of personnel is to stay away from comparisons and focus on individual potential and improvement."[14]

If a preacher fails to engage in periodic self-evaluation, he or she will acquire bad habits that are simply reinforced by practice rather than corrected. Unless we check up on ourselves, we will discover, as Deane Kemper said so well, that "these faults may persist to the detriment of the church's preaching ministry."[15]

Another objection to developing better delivery skills may seem at first quite genuine. There are preachers who fear that becoming adept communicators means resorting to manipulative methods rather than relying on the Holy Spirit to work in the hearts of the listeners. Certainly we could cite historical examples where the mind of fallen humanity has used personal speaking ability alone to stir up an audience. But this misuse of a skill should not be an argument against using it properly. It would make just as much sense to forgo the process of sermon preparation because that might cause us to depend on ourselves instead of on the Holy Spirit. Ford, in *The Ministry of the Word,* suggests that "if the preacher is to believe that his study work begun and ended in prayer is to receive the enabling power of the Divine Spirit, why must he refuse his delivery work in the pulpit that same possibility?"[16] The Holy Spirit can do His work through our faces and hands just as surely as He can through our minds.

Other preachers object to giving increased attention to delivery skills by suggesting that such an exercise distracts from the preaching event. They argue that thinking about breathing techniques or correcting faulty articulation might keep a person from concentrating on the task of explaining the text. While true, that should not keep us from working on delivery skills at other times. Practice outside the pulpit will produce benefits during the preaching event, which is not the time to be thinking about skill development. As Walter Bowie explains in *Preaching,* "These principles should belong to the preacher, not in the forefront of his attention, but in his subconscious mind, planted there—it is to be hoped—long before."[17]

Another argument against an emphasis on delivery is the contention that strong delivery will distract the audience. Some claim that attention to oral skills should be compared to acting and that actors or actresses cannot help calling attention to themselves. Having spent many years directing college drama productions, I can tell you that in actual practice it is the actor who does not pay attention to delivery skills who usually calls attention to himself. Actors are trained in delivery to draw attention to the lines spoken and the character being played rather than to the person performing the part. Preparing a narrative sermon and then delivering it poorly will definitely call attention to the speaker, but that is not an excuse for refusing to prepare diligently in order to deliver the message effectively.

It is certainly true that "to call attention to the messenger is to force attention away from the message."[18] But poor skills in delivery are far more likely to hinder the message than good skills. The best actor is not the one whose acting attracts attention; rather, he is the one who draws the audience into the story, to the place where people forget he is acting. The most skillful preacher will not call attention to his or her skill but through that skill draw attention to the story, the message from the Word.

The final and most common excuse preachers give for not being more attentive to the improvement of their delivery skills is one that the majority would hesitate to admit even to themselves. They see the self-evaluation of their public communication skills as being too discomforting and difficult to do. It requires that a person listen to his or her own preaching, something most preachers do very seldom. *Reaching People from the Pulpit* tells us that "just as self-knowledge is believed to be the most difficult of all kinds of knowledge, so listening to oneself is the most difficult of all listening."[19] We must train ourselves to listen to ourselves. And if we find that hard, then what are we doing to those who listen to us every week?

It is one thing to become interested in the improvement of delivery, but it is another to go through the examination process to determine where that improvement is needed. Occasionally an overzealous parishioner will take on the task of correcting our pulpit style. Even though we strive to remain gracious and display the fruit of the Spirit, most of us still find resentment growing and resistance building to such experiences.

We must realize that a genuine desire to improve our delivery involves more than just an evaluation of external skills. It requires us to consider our own attitude and spirit. Lowell Erdahl's words in *Better Preaching* must grab our attention like the clock at the back of the auditorium: "All preachers are themselves a vital part of their own preaching, and self-evaluation of our preaching is therefore more than careful analysis of the content of our words. It involves a searching look at ourselves as preachers and as persons."[20] We must decide if our desire to communicate God's Word is really stronger than our desire to protect ourselves from the scrutiny and hard work that a program for improvement demands. "In fact, the motivation for learning the more technical communication skills—voice production, enunciation, and articulation—is, for the authentic Christian minister, his concern for people. He communicates to help his listeners."[21]

There can be no doubt that preparing a message to preach is basic to the sermonic process. At the same time, no one can doubt the importance of giving proper attention to the manner in which that message is presented. We must seek to improve both skills. "Excellence in the preparation of sermons does not necessarily carry with it excellence in delivery, nor is excellence in delivery always a mark of good preparation and sound substance."[22] The best preaching demands both. We cannot neglect the study, but neither can we neglect the pulpit. Both are vital to the act of preaching.

3
Evaluating Yourself

■ Performing autopsies on sermons may be one of the most difficult tasks ever undertaken by a preacher. Most speakers are familiar with the practice of mulling silently over their most recent message. Every preacher learns to accept with a grain of salt the usual positive remarks at the door of the church. Some preachers even seek a spouse's opinion as to "how it went today."

Yet such brief reflections and informal comments bear as little resemblance to the self-evaluation needed to improve future pulpit communications as removing a sliver does to major surgery. Rigorous self-evaluation is not easy, but as Donald Demaray suggests, "The concern which the Holy Spirit engenders in the preacher's heart provides the motivation to develop his skills for communicating the Good News. So motivated, the disciplined preacher will give himself to constant improvement."[1]

Recognizing the need for improvement is the first step in the process. A person who has become comfortable with a particular style of delivery may be the last to realize that that style actually hinders the communication of his or her message. As soon as this realization occurs, the next step is to put into practice a disciplined program of change. Deane Kemper observes:

> For too many members of the clergy, the final and only systematic evaluation of their preaching occurs in seminary. Such instruction is not meant to last a lifetime. If tools are to be sharpened, gifts developed and skills maintained, it is the preacher's responsibility to seek out and participate in programs designed to strengthen the ministry of the Word.[2]

The exercises contained in this book hope to provide just this sort of structured program.

Before getting to the exercises, there are several things to do and keep in mind. To start you will need to set up some way to record your sermon deliveries. Audio or video recordings will work, especially if used together with other methods. You may want to consider what will work best for you. More will be said about this later.

During the process of self-criticism it is important to remember to distance yourself from each sermon you are evaluating. Do not do the exercises on Sunday afternoon. Emotional involvement is still too great so soon after the time of delivery. Lowell Erdahl in his book *Better Preaching* says, "This is not to say that we should never listen to a sermon on Sunday afternoon, but rushing to do so after every sermon may be more evidence of self-preoccupation than of serious concern for objective self-evaluation."[3] You will be better able to distance yourself from emotional involvement in the sermon if you wait at least a week after preaching before beginning your evaluation.

To get the most out of your self-evaluation, strive to listen to yourself the way others hear you. There will be a tendency for you to change your style of delivery when you know you are being taped. Since that will hinder the evaluation process, it is important to preach in your usual manner. Designing a "show" sermon for evaluation will not help you understand what your people are experiencing week after week.

Undertaking intensive self-evaluation also demands that attention be given to details. You will need to make yourself focus on one area of strength or weakness at a time. It will be necessary to watch and listen to your delivery without paying attention to the content of the message. There is a time and place for thinking about what you said, but the focus in this self-criticism process must be on how you have said it.

It is also important to make a conscious effort to put yourself in the place of the audience. Audience members see and listen through eyes and ears influenced by age, education, background, gender, and previous knowledge. Unless the speaker knows them well, it will be impossible to listen with their ears and see with their eyes. "Each kind of group has its own dynamics. What works in one setting will not necessarily succeed in another,"[4] says James Berkley in *Preaching to Convince*. The exact nature of the audience is something no classroom or teacher can impart to you, since it is constantly in flux. Your personal knowledge of your congregation will be your only guide to correctly assuming their place in the listening process. You may need to listen to a message several times from several points of view to really understand what different parts of your audience are hearing.

Recording your sermon deliveries for evaluation was mentioned earlier. There are several ways to do this. These include videotaping or digitally recording your messages, audiotaping them, writing them out, and comparative recording. All of these methods have advantages for the communicator who will use them consistently and deliberatively.

VIDEO OR DIGITAL RECORDING

Each recording you make of a sermon must be done under natural conditions. The sermons recorded should be indicative of your normal style. If you usually preach expository sermons, record an expository message rather than the occasional topical sermon. If you prefer topical preaching, don't design an expository message just because you think it might fit the evaluative criteria more closely. If you are trying the narrative method, make that the subject of your analysis. You are not competing against anyone; you are seeking to understand yourself better so your preaching can be of greater value to God and to your congregation. Record your sermons during the regular services of your church. If the videotaping of services is not done regularly, you might need to prepare the congregation by explaining in advance what is occurring. You might even need to involve some of them in doing the actual taping.

Try to obtain two recordings of each sermon. One should be a close-up that allows you to see the facial expressions used during the sermon. Set the camera on a tripod near the front of the auditorium and have an operator ready to follow you as you preach, focusing constantly on your face. One area where almost all of us can find room for improvement is in our facial expressions. Often our faces remain lifeless and dull even when our message contains life and vitality. Thomas Chadwick in his "Study of Non-Verbal Pulpit Communication" concluded, "It is as important to clear one's facial expression of ambiguities and contradictions as to clarify one's sentences."[5] This evaluation cannot be accomplished effectively if the tape is made from so far back that the preacher's facial expression remains blurred.

The second recording should be captured from about 20 feet away. It should focus on the entire person, although not the entire platform. The purpose of this tape is to show clearly the movement of the preacher, including gestures and other actions. If a preacher normally remains behind the pulpit while preaching, it would be good to position this camera to one side so that the entire body can be seen rather than being obscured by the pulpit. A person who normally remains stationary while preaching may not need someone to actually run this camera. However, someone who moves about the stage area while preaching will need an operator for this camera as well as the first one.

Although it will be possible to evaluate only one sermon at a time, it is important not to limit your evaluation to a single sermon. The first time you are recorded, you will be very aware of the cameras, a fact that may well influence your delivery. It would be best to have sermons videotaped several successive Sunday mornings. You might want to include in your evaluation sermons from other services, such as an evening service or a prayer meeting. Audience size, time of day, season of the year, health considerations, and sermon topics will all have a definite effect on your delivery. Taping multiple sermon experiences will help you collect a set of samples representing a broad range of your normal communication style. Evaluating numerous sermons instead of just one will help you spot patterns in your preaching that may or may not contribute to overall effectiveness. It is those patterns that will show you specifically how you are being perceived by those who listen regularly to your preaching, especially those junior high boys who mimic you.

Videotapes or digital recordings will be of benefit in showing you the physical aspects of your delivery style. They will help you analyze your facial expressions, eye contact, proxemics (use of space), chronemics (use of time), affect displays, illustrators, emblems, gestures, personal appearance, bodily action, and other nonverbal communication factors. You may even want to turn down the sound at times while watching the visual images. Make yourself concentrate on seeing exactly what your people are seeing while they listen to you preach.

AUDIO RECORDING

Audio recording will help the preacher focus on the vocal aspects of delivery. The advantage of listening without watching is that you will be able to concentrate on hearing rather than seeing and hearing. Be sure to tape the same four or five sermons that are being videotaped, since you will want to analyze oral as well as visual aspects of your delivery on those sermons. The various self-tests in this book will indicate whether the visual or oral recording should be used in the evaluation process.

Tapes or compact discs that contain only the oral portion of your sermons will be of benefit in evaluating vocal variety. There are basically four aspects of vocal expression that can be changed: rate, pitch, volume, and quality. Chapter 6 will elaborate on each of these. For now it's important to keep in mind that all four aspects can be improved through practice. "As is true in any activity involving skill, it is distressingly easy to acquire bad habits in sermon delivery."[6] Habits, by nature, are so familiar to a speaker that they will not identify themselves. We must make a conscious effort to recognize areas where improvements are possible.

TRANSCRIPTION

The third method used to record preaching for personal evaluation is transcription. From either the visual or audio recording, have someone transcribe the sermon onto paper. Be careful that every sound is written down, including verbal fillers such as "uh," "um," "OK," "er," and other such expressions. Instruct the transcriber not to correct grammar, finish incomplete sentences, or otherwise change the message. Your purpose in this exercise will be to observe the exact form your message takes when it reaches the ears of the listeners. Often when we listen to ourselves, we ignore fillers and we complete thoughts that were actually incomplete. When we are faced with a transcript, it is harder to avoid the reality of the sounds that come out of our mouths. Al Fasol says, "Personally, transcribing a portion of my sermons and analyzing the transcription as described is the single most expeditious way of improving the quality of my preaching that I have ever done."[7]

Transcribing sermons will also facilitate an evaluation of word choice. Extemporaneous preaching has the great advantage of immediacy when compared to manuscript preaching. Few preachers can write out a sermon and then deliver it in a manner that sounds fresh and direct. One reason for that is the distinct difference between written and oral language. Writing requires careful attention to sentence construction, accurate punctuation, and grammatical structure to convey meaning. In contrast, the meaning of spoken words depends on voice inflection. The great advantage of manuscript preparation lies in the opportunity to choose appropriate words, especially when a person learns to write in an oral style. "Without this drudgery of the pen, we are apt to become loose and sloppy in style. Unconsciously also, we tend to drop into well-beaten grooves both of thought and phrasing, and repeat ourselves,"[8] writes James Black in *The Mystery of Preaching*.

Preparing a word-for-word transcription after preaching will help you analyze extemporaneous word choices and determine how much of the discipline of manuscript preparation needs to be practiced for sermonic improvement. Word choice involves both content and delivery, since it grows out of our study but occurs at the moment of communication. The words we choose to use can be one of the most effective or ineffective means of emphasizing our thoughts.

COMPARATIVE RECORDING

One other method you may want to include is an oral or visual re-cording of yourself in normal conversation. Since you are already having someone record your preaching, ask that person to include on the tape a recording of the earlier part of the service when you greet the congrega-tion and give announcements. Most speakers tend to be quite natural during those activities.

Recent communication theory suggests that the most effective form of public address involves heightened conversation. People in the audience should feel that the speaker is addressing them directly as if conversing with them one on one. Comparing a tape of your normal conversation with one of your preaching style may help you determine if there are great differences in the way you speak in conversation and the way you speak from the pulpit. It may reveal tendencies toward a preacher's tone that inhibits directness in communication between you and the listener. An ability to make people feel that you are talking directly with them even though you are addressing an audience can be an invaluable aid in increasing pulpit effectiveness.

After recording a variety of sermon presentations, the next step in the process involves identifying specific strengths and weaknesses. The fol-lowing chapters will provide a series of self-tests with which that analy-sis can be accomplished. Although it may seem time-consuming, the greatest profit will come if you will listen to a complete sermon or even several sermons while answering the questions on a single self-test. Pat-terns in preaching are of greater importance than individual slips of the tongue or momentary lapses of memory. Just once substituting "Noah" for "Jonah" in a message is not a great problem. But continually substituting a "t" sound in place of a "th" sound could significantly affect the ability of your audience to understand what you are saying.

Try to answer the questions on the self-tests according to what you see and hear on the recordings rather than according to what you thought you said or how you thought you looked. Your task is to achieve the goal Robert Burns desired in his poem "To a Louse," which he subtitled "On Seeing One on a Lady's Bonnet at Church."

> *O wad some Power the giftie gie us*
> *To see oursels as ithers see us!*[9]

After identifying strengths and weaknesses, you will be able to isolate individual practices that require improvement. Each self-test is accompanied by a set of exercises that will help you practice and modify your vocal and physical delivery. These exercises should be used outside of the pulpit. The focus during preaching must always be on the communication of the text, not on the delivery of the speaker. That is not the time to be working on various delivery techniques. As Erdahl says, "Periodic self-examination helps to free us from perpetual self-preoccupation."[10] A consistent practice outside the pulpit will improve sermon delivery over a period of time. Trying to consciously practice exercises while in the pulpit will result in a self-consciousness that will not lead to improvement.

Evaluating your sermons does not necessarily mean that you will need to change anything about the way you preach. Careful analysis may simply confirm the effectiveness of the sermon style with which you are comfortable. If weaknesses surface, then certainly the desire to handle the Word of God effectively would compel a person to look for appropriate remedies. James Black expresses the desire of every preacher when he says, "Our aim is to touch and move the will, mind, conscience and heart of all our people."[11] Failure to strive for the best in the area of platform delivery may keep a person from accomplishing the goal of preaching, that is, reaching the heart of the listener.

As part of an expository preaching course, I would sit down with each student to watch a videotape of one of his or her sermons to help the student in the process of self-evaluation. An experience with two students who came to watch sermons on the same day may help to illustrate the value this practice can have in the life of a preacher.

The first student had started class with a good background in communications and had maintained an A average throughout the semester. Overall he was adept at writing outlines and had developed good delivery skills. During the video evaluation, however, he was constantly asking questions concerning methods of improvement. Any suggestion I made was written down and discussed in an open, positive fashion. He was already in the process of reworking his classroom presentation for future use. He had noted several places on his own that he thought needed improvement, and he sought my advice on those changes. During the session, we discovered together several illustrations that he determined to pursue and develop for when he used the message the next time. When we were finished, he spoke appreciatively of the session in a genuine fashion, saying how beneficial it had been to meet and evaluate his sermon.

The second student, although likewise friendly, obviously had a much better estimation of his own abilities than I did. He had been a consistent C student throughout the semester. As we watched his sermon, every suggestion I made was met with a defense of why he had done it the way he did. Even when I explained that something had been done well, but could be improved, he continued to defend the original fashion in which he had preached. There was no focus on reworking the message. I'm certain that if the outline were ever used again, it would be used without noticeable change and therefore without improvement. There were no questions on his part during the entire session. We discovered nothing together. My comments were received, and possibly understood, but I doubt they were ever applied.

The value of self-evaluation lies in the application that is made of the discovery. The self-tests will aid in the process of evaluation. The exercises will aid in the process of improvement. Together they will be one means of charting a personal path to greater effectiveness in the communication of the gospel of Jesus Christ. Properly applied, they will be of great help to a preacher in telling the "story." It is certainly true that we cannot preach a greater message, but we can certainly strive to do a better job of preaching that message for His glory.

4

Improving Emphasis Through Word Choice

■ Words are the raw lumber from which sermons are crafted. The final product will only be as beautiful and functional as the materials from which it was made. If you begin with plywood, you will end with a plywood box. If you begin with oak and cedar, you can construct a hope chest for the soul. Both boxes will function as containers, but how listeners choose to use them will vary greatly, and the value they place upon them will be vastly different.

Words are vehicles carrying our ideas to the minds of others. They can gallop like the Pony Express or plod like Old Dobbin. They can blast like a steam locomotive or purr like a well-tuned Mercedes. They can be "quick, and powerful, and sharper than any two-edged sword, piercing even to the dividing asunder of soul and spirit, and of the joints and marrow" (Heb. 4:12).

The preacher should fall in love with words. They should become his or her sought-after daily companions, friends, hobby, and occupation. "The theme of a minister's use of words is literally boundless. It deserves the lifelong diligence of every minister,"[1] says Halfold Luccock in *The Minister's Workshop.* As Humpty Dumpty told Alice just before he fell off the wall, "When I make a word do a lot of work like that, I always pay it extra."[2] The purpose for this love affair with words must not be self-promotion. Instead, it must be for furthering our overall goal of improving communication. Jay Adams writes in *Pulpit Speech,* "The counter-pressure of language means that wrongly chosen words thrust back at us and reshape our thought and misshape our communication; sometimes quite seriously. Style, then, tends to add and subtract."[3]

As those who handle the Word of God, we must be certain that our word choice adds to the total impact of the message rather than subtracting from it. The actual creation of the story we will eventually share with our congregation begins at the level of the individual words from which we will craft our story. For the "story" teller, words must be quarried from the richest mines and harvested from the choicest vineyards.

In the following words, Halford Luccock vividly captures the futility of speaking without giving diligent thought to word choice:

How many words will a man speak in the course of a forty-year ministry? . . . Suppose he is a modern minister who preaches once a Sunday a thirty-minute sermon. Call that 4500 words, allowing 150 words a minute. Give him a four-week vacation and two Sundays away. That makes 46 times 4500 words, or 207,000 words a year. Multiply by forty years and you get a total of 8,280,000 words. . . . Think of the endless other occasions when the minister speaks. . . . These will lift the total to well over ten million. Then think how truly terrible it would be . . . to utter that many words, . . . without ever having undergone any arduous discipline to master the ways of words—as precision instruments of thought. . . . Yet many a preacher has avoided the costly toil. . . . And the churchgoing of many of the faithful has been truly a sacrifice, in that they have been bored nigh unto death by the steady drizzle of the same words and . . . outworn phrases. Surely there is a special meaning for preachers in the warning that for every idle word we shall stand in judgment. There are many kinds of idle words; one kind, surely, is that which comes from complacent idleness rather than from toil over language.[4]

Working to improve oral delivery will be pointless unless we first give attention to word choice. The proper inflection of the wrong words will not increase clarity; it will only serve to more effectively confuse the hearer. Just as content is the basis for determining delivery style, so must it be for determining word choice. "There can be no clear speaking without clear thinking,"[5] was W. E. Sangster's advice. The problem comes when our clear thinking in the study does not translate into clear speaking in the pulpit. Too often preachers are content to use the first words that come to mind at the time of extemporaneous delivery, rather than working diligently so that the mind will produce the best words with the greatest potential impact.

The first words that come to mind are often archaic, obscure, and dull and will never work to carry the thoughts of a sermon. The ideas of Scripture deserve to be carried in 747s, and instead we send them aloft in unmanned gliders, hoping they will stay up long enough to reach their destination. Archaic language often results from trying to use the constructions of old English familiar to those who have read extensively from the King James Bible. Saying "divers" instead of "diverse" because that is the way it is spelled in the KJV will not help an audience understand your message. We must constantly think of how our audience is hearing the words we choose.

Language is often dull because we have not taken the time to enrich it with figures of speech as Jesus did. He talked about men who were like cities of light shining on the hilltops. He described one of the rulers of his day as a fox. Hypocrites were like tombs full of rotting bones painted white on the outside. His language was always vivid and never dull.

Language is often unclear because we have not thought deeply about a subject before discussing it. We have been content to think in clichés and familiar Christian phrases without ever asking what those phrases mean to a person who has no religious background. Sometimes we even repeat phrases from Scripture without a clear idea of how we would express that idea if we had to rephrase it in our own words. We really don't understand any phrase until we can communicate the same concept in words of our own choosing.

Those who do think deeply about the Scriptures often face the contrasting problem in their word choice. They discover technical words, rich in content, words such as "propitiation" and "consubstantiation." Properly understood, such words can shed tremendous light on a subject in a short time. While there is definitely a place for technical, theological language—and our study would be impoverished indeed without such terms—their place is not in the pulpit. "The great biblical, theological terms must be used, but not without explanation, nor should they be used in profusion,"[6] warns Jay Adams. Sermons are not lectures; they are meals served in such a way that the listener desires to eat and live.

Abstract language occurs often in theological education, and there is a great danger that the preacher will be content to simply repeat those words rather than make them concrete. Concrete language involves the world where we live, words that contain the ability to make us see and feel rather than just think. Paul Scott Wilson illustrates the difference by quoting from Owen Thomas on the subject of scriptural inspiration.

Though not everyone may agree with Thomas's viewpoint, the selection is typical of theological, abstract language:

> This theory of verbal inspiration and of revelation as the communication of propositional truths from God to humanity does not fit the facts of the Bible. It makes the words of the Bible the locus of revelation rather than the events described in the Bible. The words of the Bible are the record of events and the interpretation of them as events in which God is acting. Faith or the reception of revelation in the Bible is clearly not the acceptance of supernaturally communicated propositions but rather trust in and obedience to the living God who confronts humanity in the events of the Bible.[7]

In contrast to the abstract language of Owen, Wilson presents his own version of the same material, expressed in more concrete language:

> When the Bible was written, God did not decide to lie down in lines on a page and squeeze into particular words lined up on that page, that we could then dust off and lift up and have them turn back into God's truth. God always has been found where the action is happening, in the midst of human affairs, particularly where people are in despair and needing a help that is beyond themselves. The Bible records crucial events, but it is the living God who speaks through them illumining the events of all times. It is God who in this manner shows us who God is, and it is this God who meets us now and gives us all the faith to carry on.[8]

We cannot and must not eliminate all abstract terms from preaching. To do so would be to rob ourselves of some wonderful, biblical language. But as God does in His Word, we must constantly be striving to present abstract, theological language in ways that bring it into the consciousness of our listeners.

A great example of the power of word choice occurs in the Book of 2 Samuel. Absalom has just rebelled against his father, David, and has to decide whether to pursue the king as he flees across the Jordan. Two advisers, Ahithophel and Hushai, give the rebel son conflicting advice. Read the two speeches in 2 Sam. 17:1-3 and verses 7-13, and then consider Warren Wiersbe's insightful comments:

> In modern terms, Ahithophel used a cerebral "left brain" approach and Hushai, a visceral "right brain" approach. Absalom *heard* what Ahithophel was saying, but he *saw* and *felt* what Hushai was saying. Ahithophel's counsel was wise, but it was rejected, and this led to his

humiliation and death. Hushai's counsel was weak in military strategy, but it was accepted and led to Absalom's defeat.[9]

Our goal as preachers should not be to have bad advice accepted simply on the basis of our excellent choice of words. But with the goal of communicating God's own message, we would be well served to give diligent attention to the principles Hushai used to get his message across. Our task of preaching deserves persistent attention to the demanding task of effective word choice.

AUDIENCE ADAPTATION

Words produce understanding only when their meanings are shared by both the communicator and the audience. The most obvious illustration of this would be the foreign traveler who speaks only English while trying to talk to an audience that understands only Bengali. The finest delivery techniques will have only limited effectiveness because there is no shared language.

When speaking in English to those who understand English, however, the same problem remains. Some words will have different meanings, both connotative and denotative, for the audience. In fact, some words will produce different understandings in various members of the same audience. Other words will be understood but will have greater or less effectiveness than alternate choices that the speaker could have made. The goal of the public communicator should be to present a message in words that will have the greatest possible impact upon the immediate audience. To do that, a sermon must be adapted to fit the demographics of that audience. We must tell the story of Scripture in words that can be understood.

Every time a person preaches, the audience will be slightly different, even if preaching regularly in the same church. Although general conclusions can be reached about a typical audience, one of the tasks of every minister is to become so well acquainted with people that he or she knows the very words that will enable them to gain a greater understanding of the Word of God.

Information concerning an audience can be obtained from a variety of sources. If you are preaching to a totally new congregation, you may have to depend on your contact person for some idea of who will be present. But if you preach regularly to the same people, you will be able to learn by direct observation. In addition to seeing them, however, a minister must learn to listen to them. That involves getting into their homes, sharing fellowship with them outside of church activities, visiting their places of employment, and allowing them to share with you what they are thinking. It will mean gaining an understanding of the cultural environment influencing them between Sundays. Some pastors meet regularly with a small-group cross-section of their audience to discuss sermon topics before they are preached. Words you have discovered in your historical research that may be unfamiliar can be given a test run to help you determine how much explanation will be needed during the sermon.

Data collection may also help a preacher analyze the audience. By the time a minister has completed college and seminary and served a church for several years, he or she may have lost contact with the workaday world where most people live. It is good to be reminded statistically of what that world is like, even if the figures don't completely match the profile of those who are attending your church. Joey Faucette offers the following statistical analysis:

Consider the hypothetical situation of a congregation of five hundred adults who represent a cross-section of the American population. Of these five hundred parishioners:

—25 have been hospitalized in the past for a major mental illness.

—24 are alcoholics.

—50 are severely handicapped by neurotic conflicts.

—100 are afflicted by moderate neurotic symptoms.

—115 would answer "yes" to the question, "Have you ever felt you were going to have a nervous breakdown?"

—70 have sought professional help for a personal or marital problem in the past.

—1 will attempt suicide every other year.

—8 will be involved in a serious crime.

—Fewer than one-half of those persons married would rate their marriage as "very happy."

While this hypothetical situation is unlikely to be true for every congregation, it serves to illustrate the scope and depth of human need among the people who assemble for worship each Sunday.[10]

A typical audience analysis would include such items as average age and age range, gender composition, cultural variety, socioeconomic composition, occupations, religious orientation, political preferences, and the degree of homogeneity or heterogeneity of the crowd. In addition to those basic considerations, a pastor will want to know the specific life tasks and needs that are facing his listeners. Faucette explains, "The Bible is filled with stories of adults at virtually all stages of life. Studying the lives and situations of biblical persons acquaints the incarnational pastor with the source materials for his sermons."[11]

In the following self-test you will analyze your own sermons to see if there is evidence of audience adaptation. To prepare for taking the self-test, watch one of your sermons on videotape while consciously attempting to see and listen from the viewpoint of various individuals you knew were present that day. Choose a variety of individuals, differing in age, gender, cultural background, and occupation, and try to see the sermon through their eyes.

Self-Test on Audience Adaptation

1. From the viewpoint of an eight-year-old boy, answer the following questions:
   a. What did I know about this topic before the sermon began?
   b. Did I have any interest in this topic before the sermon began?
   c. Was my attitude toward this topic good, bad, or indifferent?
   d. What was said during the sermon that interested me in this topic?
   e. What was said that would show me how this topic applies to my life?
   f. Were there any illustrations that particularly grabbed my interest?
   g. Did the preacher ever explain any words that I didn't understand?
   h. Did I feel as if the entire sermon was directed at my parents?
   i. Did I think the preacher cared that I was there?
   j. Would I have any interest in talking to the preacher more about this topic?

2. From the viewpoint of a 16-year-old girl, answer the following questions:
   a. Was the sermon on a subject about which my friends and I have ever talked?
   b. Was the subject one I have wondered about, even if I've never talked to anyone about it?
   c. Did anything the preacher said during the first two minutes of the sermon make me want to know more about this subject?

      d. Did the preacher talk about any of the activities I have been involved in over the past week?

      e. Did the sermon make me feel as if the preacher understood how I feel about this subject?

      f. Were there any stories or illustrations in the sermon that reflected the youth culture where I live?

      g. Were any words used that specifically related to girls instead of guys?

      h. Would I have any interest in talking to the preacher further about this subject?

3. From the viewpoint of a new mother in her late 20s, answer the following questions:

      a. Have my husband and I ever talked previously about the subject of this sermon?

      b. Was the subject one we should have discussed but have been avoiding?

      c. If I had known the subject before I came to church, would I have been anxious to hear it discussed?

      d. What was said in the first few minutes of the message that convinced me I had a real need to learn about this topic?

      e. Was anything said in this sermon that made me believe that the preacher understands my life situation?

      f. Were any illustrations used that related to incidents that have been a part of my experience during the last week?

      g. Did I feel as if the words of the sermon were addressed mainly to my husband?

      h. Do I think the preacher would understand my attitude toward this subject if I discussed it with him or her sometime in the future?

4. From the viewpoint of a retired widower, 78 years of age, answer the following questions:

      a. In my previous thinking about this subject, have I viewed it as primarily a theological topic or a practical topic?

      b. Was anything said in the first few minutes of the sermon that convinced me this topic would be important to me in my retirement?

      c. Did I feel as if I were listening to the preacher talk to other people about their problems?

      d. Did the preacher use any specific words or illustrations that brought back memories?

e. Were words used that made me feel useless or unnecessary in the total life of the congregation, as if this message were only for those who could still be active in the Lord's work?

f. Did I feel as if the message were mainly directed at my children?

g. Do I really feel that the preacher would want to discuss this topic further with me sometime in the future and listen to what I have to say?

5. From the viewpoint of an unsaved businessman in his mid-40s, answer the following questions:

a. Would I read a magazine article on this subject?

b. Would I read more than the first two paragraphs of a magazine article on this subject if the first two paragraphs were identical to the first two minutes of this sermon?

c. Do I think of this subject as "religious" in nature or "secular" in nature?

d. Are there words in this sermon that everyone around me seems to understand, but which say nothing to me?

e. Is there anything in this sermon that shows the preacher understands the world of work in which I live?

f. Does the preacher ever stop to explain his or her religious terminology?

g. Do I feel as if the preacher cares about my questions and doubts concerning this topic?

h. What do I think would be this preacher's reaction if I called this week and argued with him or her about what was said in this sermon?

SCORING: Look back over your answers. If necessary, repeat the self-test for sermons on a variety of topics. Are you favoring certain components of your total audience in how you craft the words of your message? Are you ignoring other potential listeners? Complete the following exercises to improve your ability to communicate with all those who listen to you preach.

Exercises for Improvement of Audience Adaptation

1. Below is a general sermon topic and three hypothetical audiences to which that sermon might be delivered. Write a brief paragraph explaining how you might adjust the proposition (theme), development,

and application of your message according to the religious background of each audience.

Topic: Christ as Our Great High Priest in the Line of Melchizedek

Audience No. 1: Adult Sunday School class, church members

Audience No. 2: State university religion class, 80 percent unbelievers, 20 percent believers from a variety of church backgrounds

Audience No. 3: Adult Sunday School class, new believers

2. Read the following paragraph. Then rewrite the paragraph in language that would be age appropriate for each of the hypothetical audiences described below.

The atonement is described as a work of priestly mediation which reconciles God to men, —notice here that the term "reconciliation" has its usual sense of removing enmity, not from the offending, but from the offended party: —a sin offering, presented on behalf of transgressors: —a propitiation, which satisfies the demands of violated holiness; . . . These passages, taken together, show that Christ's death is demanded by God's attributes of justice, or holiness, if sinners are to be saved.[12]

Audience No. 1: Teen Bible study in a public high school

Audience No. 2: New converts Sunday School class, 50 percent men, 50 percent women

Audience No. 3: Sunday evening sermon, 60 percent adult believers, 40 percent children

3. Choose an illustration from one of your sermons. You will need to use the transcript of your sermon for this exercise. Determine the exact point in the Scripture text that you intended to illustrate. Then choose a new illustration that makes the same point but would appeal directly to the following segments of your audience.
   a. An 8-year-old boy
   b. A 16-year-old girl
   c. A new mother in her late 20s
   d. An unsaved businessman in his mid-40s
   e. A retired widower, 78 years of age

4. Paraphrase the following scriptures in a way that would make them understandable to a college-educated man with no prior Bible knowledge. Write down your paraphrase and work carefully to choose words that communicate the meaning of the text without repeating the words of the text.
   a. "And immediately there fell from his eyes as it had been scales:

and he received sight forthwith, and arose, and was baptized" (Acts 9:18).

b. "If we confess our sins, he is faithful and just to forgive us our sins, and to cleanse us from all unrighteousness" (1 John 1:9).

c. "For the earnest expectation of the creature waiteth for the manifestation of the sons of God" (Rom. 8:19).

d. "For if, when we were enemies, we were reconciled to God by the death of his Son, much more, being reconciled, we shall be saved by his life" (Rom. 5:10).

e. "Let mine adversaries be clothed with shame, and let them cover themselves with their own confusion, as with a mantle" (Ps. 109:29).

f. "Thou shalt fear the LORD thy God, and serve him, and shalt swear by his name" (Deut. 6:13).

EVALUATING SERMON INTRODUCTIONS

The introduction to a sermon may be, from the standpoint of total effectiveness, the most important part of the entire message. Like the opening sentences of a newspaper article, the opening paragraph of a novel, and the lead-in to the evening news, an introduction captures attention and focuses it on what is to come. It should arouse curiosity without giving away the plot. According to David Buttrick in *Homiletic Moves and Structures,* "Introductions should not tell a congregation where we are going or, worse, how we are going to go ahead of time. Instead, introductions provide initial focus; they bring into consciousness the 'scene' of the sermon before there is any moving around within the scene."[13] In a narrative sermon the introduction could be compared to the first scene of a play or the first paragraph of a short story.

During informal conversation, we react adversely to people who jump right into a subject without warning. A young man who has walked a college campus for four years will not be well received if he approaches a girl he has never talked to in all that time with, "I think August 2 would be a good day for our wedding." The more important the subject, the more time we need to provide for adjustment on the part of our listener. Just because a person has been sitting through a half-hour song service does not mean he or she is ready to listen to you talk about your topic of choice.

This introductory matter is not for the purpose of avoiding the subject until a few empty sentences have been exchanged, however. Too many sermons begin with just such useless patter, followed by comments such as, "That didn't have anything to do with what I'm going to be talking about." The introduction to a sermon has the specific purpose of capturing the attention of an audience, focusing it on a particular subject, and convincing the audience that they should listen to this person talk about that subject.

Capturing attention is not really very hard to do. Setting off a firecracker, standing on your head, or riding down the aisle on a white stallion would capture attention. The speaker is not trying to capture attention for himself or herself but rather trying to draw the attention of the audience to a particular subject. That is why word choice becomes so important in the preparation of your first few sentences. You have one or maybe two minutes to interest people in a subject you want them to think about for a half-hour or more.

So we use an introduction to focus attention on a topic and also prepare the listener for a favorable and intelligent reception of the truth. With many topics there is background material that an audience needs in order to understand the development of the speaker's ideas. The amount of background material may depend on the audience's previous knowledge, which can only be determined by audience analysis. Because context plays such a large part in expository preaching, some preachers tend to dwell extensively on background material as a prerequisite to every message. Often this results in an introduction satisfactory to the intellectual curiosity of those whose minds are already engaged by the subject but fails to arouse the interest of anyone else.

Preparation for narrative preaching brings the preacher into contact with reams of interesting historical and cultural materials. With this comes the danger of trying to share all of that background before starting the story. A good introduction must fulfill two purposes—attract attention and provide necessary background. If it errs too far in either direction, some part of the audience will be lost before the sermon has even begun.

Another component of an effective introduction involves the relationship between the audience and the speaker. An audience needs to be sufficiently acquainted with the preacher for them to willingly accept his or her arguments or at least listen to those arguments before drawing conclusions. A speaker must obtain the goodwill of the listener. A preacher who preaches regularly to the same people has other means of obtaining or losing goodwill. What people thought about you at the end of the previous message will affect their willingness to listen on subsequent occasions. But every new topic also brings with it the need to convince listeners that you are qualified to address it.

Having to introduce yourself to the audience does not mean that every sermon must begin with personal stories. In fact, the introduction is probably not a good place for personal illustrations. Buttrick cautions against the practice when he writes, "As a preacher, you are attempting at the outset of a sermon to focus congregational consciousness on an image, or an idea, or a scriptural passage, or whatever. But, by speaking of yourself, inevitably the congregation will focus on you. There is no way to prevent the split."[14] The introduction should be crafted in such a way that the audience sees the speaker's qualifications through his or her word choice and not through attention drawn to his or her person, background, or achievements.

Usually a discussion about introductions focuses on the types of materials suitable for introducing a sermon: quotations, illustrations, anecdotes, songs, poetry, reference to the occasion, and so on. The following self-test will concern itself instead with the effectiveness of the chosen materials in relation to the words used to craft the opening sentences. Use written transcripts of your sermons, along with video or digital recordings, to evaluate the effectiveness of your sermon introductions.

Self-Test for Evaluating Sermon Introductions

1. Choose at least five different sermons you have preached and recorded. Write down the requested information from each sermon, and then answer the questions as indicated. You will want to use the transcripts of your sermons for this exercise.

   a. Write down the very first word spoken when you arrived on the platform to begin preaching each sermon.

      (1) _____

      (2) _____

      (3) _____

      (4) _____

      (5) _____

   b. Write down the complete first phrase or sentence spoken from the pulpit at the beginning of each sermon.

      (1) _____

    (2) _____

    (3) _____

    (4) _____

    (5) _____

  c. Answer the following questions while considering the words and sentences recorded above.

    (1) Are any of the five words in "a" identical?

        Yes   No

    (2) Do any of the messages begin with the word "turn"?

        Yes   No

    (3) Is one or more of the sentences in "b" a question?

        Yes   No

    (4) Do your sentences capture attention when standing alone?

        Yes   No

    (5) Is each first sentence directly related to the sermon topic?

        Yes   No

    (6) Does each first sentence begin in the present tense?

        Yes   No

    (7) Is more than one of the sentences compound/complex?

        Yes   No

    (8) Are any of the beginnings phrases or sentence fragments?

        Yes   No

2. Listen carefully to one of your sermon introductions, and then read the transcript of the same introduction while considering the answers to the following questions.

  a. Do I ever talk about matters unrelated to the topic of the message before actually beginning a specific introduction that leads to that topic?

    Yes   No

  b. Do my introductions begin with a larger field of general knowledge and then focus attention on an area of specific knowledge?

    Yes   No

  c. Do my introductions assume that the audience is already thinking about the sermon topic of the day?

    Yes   No

  d. Does my introduction include a summary of the sermon outline?

    Yes   No

e. Do my introductions extend beyond about 15 sentences?

      Yes   No

f. Are my introductions shorter than about 7 sentences?

      Yes   No

g. Are the first 2 sentences of the introductions loaded with adjectives?

      Yes   No

h. Is there a reference in the introduction to the text from which I will be preaching?

      Yes   No

i. Did the introduction contain biblical background material unnecessary to an understanding of the sermon topic?

      Yes   No

j. Did the introduction contain any sentences that could be eliminated without changing the total impact of the message?

      Yes   No

k. Do any of the introductions include questions asking the listener to think about his or her own experiences?

      Yes   No

l. Do any of the introductions contain humorous remarks or jokes?

      Yes   No

SCORING:

1. Starting with 1c, give yourself 1 point for each of the answers listed below.

    No. 1—Yes

    No. 2—Yes

    No. 3—Yes

    No. 4—No

    No. 5—No

    No. 6—No

    No. 7—Yes

    No. 8—No

2. Give yourself 1 point for each of the following answers.

a. Yes

b. No

c. Yes

d. Yes

e. Yes

f. Yes

g. Yes

h. No

i. Yes

j. Yes

k. Yes

l. Yes

If you scored more than 4 points on this self-test, you would do well to pay close attention to your word choice in the preparation of your introductions. Use the following exercises to facilitate improvement in the areas of variety, imagery, focus, capturing attention, clarity, simplicity, and oral style.

Exercises for the Improvement of Introductions

One of the greatest gifts a preacher can present to an audience is variety. Introductions should not be interchangeable; that is, each one should fit distinctly the message it prefaces. So if each message is different, each introduction should also be different. Choose from among many available methods the best way to introduce each specific sermon.

Narrative Introductions

Example: "Miriam went to hear that new preacher last week. The one named Haggai. I didn't go. I was just too busy. But I might as well have gone. All I've heard this entire week is 'Haggai this,' and 'Haggai that.' The strange thing about it is that I have no idea what the fellow looks like. She doesn't talk about what he wore or how old he was or what his voice sounded like. All she can talk about is what he said. When I tried to ask about those other things, she just shook her head and repeated, 'It was like hearing the voice of God.'

"You know, it's been a long time since I've heard the voice of God. Don't tell Miriam, but I might just go listen to this fellow Haggai if he ever preaches another message." (From an introduction to Haggai's second message in Hag. 1:12-15)

1. How do you introduce another person? What do you notice about him or her? What do you talk about when you tell about the meeting? Write a paragraph in which you introduce a biblical character through the eyes of someone who just met that person.

2. Now write a paragraph in which the biblical character introduces himself or herself to a stranger. Have the character explain who he or she is and also who he or she is not.

3. Think how you could use a narrative introduction for one of your messages you have been analyzing. Write a narration that captures attention and leads to the text for that specific sermon.

Descriptive Introductions

Example: It began as a quiet procession—Jesus and a few followers trudging the dusty road from Bethany to Jerusalem. Then Jesus mounted a donkey, not because He was tired, but because He knew it was time, God's time, to make an announcement to the city of Zion. The disciples started to shout praise. Word spread. Crowds gathered. The multitudes, crowded inside the city walls for Passover, spilled out the gates, and everywhere could be heard the same question, "Have you seen the King?" Have you?

1. Choose one of your sermons that starts with a Bible event, and describe the setting in terms of what can be seen.

2. Rewrite the same event in terms of what can be heard. Shut your eyes and listen to the action in your mind, focusing on the sounds of the setting.

3. Place yourself in the scene and describe the event with words that express what can be touched. Feel with your hands, your feet, and your skin. Notice temperature, texture, moisture, size, and weight.

Specific Time Introductions

Example: It started at 11 A.M. on September 6, 1997, and around the world more than 1 billion people sat in front of their television sets to watch. The funeral of Princess Diana attracted a larger crowd than any other event in modern history. Reactions to her death were many and varied. Rita Traschel, a reporter for the *Wilmington News Journal,* captured the feelings of many with this statement, "Her death was so shockingly pointless." But the most poignant message was contained in the simple card that rode on top of the casket with the single word, "Mummy." Perhaps the reason Diana's death captured the attention of so many people lies in the fact that death is, after all, the common denominator. Death at 36 when you are young and rich and beautiful seems shockingly pointless. But death at any age robs someone of a "Mummy" or "Dad-

dy" or child. If we are to be like Christ, then certainly we need to understand His reaction to that experience which all of us will face—the loss
of a loved one.

1. Choose a modern-day event that parallels the opening action in one
    of your sermons. Learn specific details concerning the occasion, and
    write an introduction that focuses on the time of the event.

2. Take a biblical story and write it in the present tense. Then match it
    with an incident concerning someone in the present day. For exam-
    ple: The challenges of Goliath and the boasting of the neighborhood
    bully. See if you can start with the contemporary story (the bully) and
    make a smooth transition back into the biblical incident (Goliath).

3. Begin your story by tying together the recent past and the distant
    past. Use the basic formula "He did as he had done." For example:
    "Paul preached as Moses had preached in the wilderness, hurling the
    Word of God down on their heads. He preached as Elijah had
    preached, calling down fire from heaven. Paul preached as Ezekiel
    had preached, opening before them visions of the glory of God."

4. Take one of your introductions and change the tense, present to past
    or vice versa. Does it work as well? Does it work better? If you always
    begin your sermons in the past tense, consider the occasional use of
    the present when it is appropriate.

Quotation Introductions

Example: Our world is filled with strange ideas of what it means to
fail and to succeed. A basketball team can be selected for the NCAA
Tournament, win every game except the final, lose that on a come-from-
behind desperation shot, and be considered a failure. Muhammad Ali
once described his success in his chosen field this way, "It's just a job.
Grass grows. Birds fly. Waves pound the sand. I beat people up."[15]

1. Try reading the above example with the direct quotation coming first.
    Does it have the same impact when you don't know who is being
    quoted? Try leaving out the words "Muhammad Ali once described his
    success in his chosen field this way." What happens to the effect of
    the quote? Start reading at the words "Muhammad Ali." Is the quote
    as effective without the opening remarks about success and failure?

2. Find a quotation that would fit one of the sermons you are analyzing.
    Place it into a written setting that prepares the audience to hear the

quotation through judicious word choice. Be sure to include language that identifies the speaker.

3. Look back over your sermon introductions, and notice how you have made reference to the text for the day. Rewrite one of the introductions using a short reference to a key phrase from the sermon text as if it were a quotation. Don't give a specific Scripture reference, but instead look for a way to identify it with the author of the text while focusing attention on the sermon topic.

Historical Introductions

Example: Everything that could go wrong, had gone wrong. Congress in the winter of 1777 let soldiers enlist for two months at a time. At the end of their enlistment thousands would leave Valley Forge on a single day. Others enlisted only for the bonus and deserted before night fell. Congress refused to provide supplies of food, clothing, and ammunition needed by the Continental Army. A group of army officers and members of Congress were plotting to remove Washington from his position as general of the army. And what did General Washington do when the bottom had fallen out of his world? He prayed. In the cold of that terrible winter, soldiers would often see their commander in chief on his knees in the early morning hours, pouring out his petitions to the God of all nations.

1. This introduction begins with a simple truth. Write five more sentences like that. Examples: "It was the saddest story he had ever heard." "I had never heard a shorter sermon."

2. Write the story of Mary and Joseph beginning with a line like this: "Their story really touched my heart as they stood at the door of my inn."

3. Choose a historical incident that parallels the opening truth of one of the sermons you are analyzing. Tell the story with enough specific detail to bring it to life for your listeners.

4. Rewrite the example above in dialogue, having George Washington tell his own story. Write it in first person. Then write it in third person, adding descriptive details concerning what Washington does while he is talking. Which do you like best?

CONCLUSIONS

Sermons should burn with such intensity that this question should be on the lips of every person in the audience when the conclusion is reached, "Brothers, what shall we do?" (Acts 2:37, NIV). A sermon is not designed simply to reach the mind; it must reach the heart as well. Although application should not be limited to the conclusion, it is at that point in the sermon where a definite transition must be made from the intellect to the heart. "A biblical sermon must both explain and apply God's truth. If you want explanations without application, you attend a theological lecture,"[16] says Warren Wiersbe. An effective conclusion will take the listener from the place of mental agreement to the place of responsive action.

Because of the importance of motivating the audience to action, a conclusion should never contain an apology. Confession may be good for the soul, but it isn't a good way to conclude a message. Feelings of inadequacy plague every speaker from time to time, but it will not help your audience to say something like, "I know this hasn't been much, but maybe the Lord will bless it anyway." It is possible that such a remark is simply thinly veiled pride. The focus of the conclusion must always be on the response of the people to the text, not on their response to the preacher.

In the narrative sermon the conclusion should not be like the moral at the end of a fable by Aesop. Don't allow the story to come to an end and then step aside and offer an explanation. Conclude in the same voices and with the same energy characterizing the story itself.

Conclusions must not be interchangeable between sermons. Variety in the methods used to conclude sermons is just as important as variety in how they are introduced. Familiarity with a style of sermon conclusion will usually prompt an audience to begin preparations for departure. In one sense, your conclusion should be a surprise. You want the listeners to be so engrossed in what is being said that they hardly notice the sermon is drawing to an end.

For your conclusion to accomplish this, it must be one of the first parts of the message you prepare. That is not to say its final form will be written first, but a preacher must know the goal before seeking ways to that goal. You don't have to restate the proposition, or scriptural theme, as a part of the conclusion, but the conclusion should aim at reinforcing it in a vivid, forceful, personal manner.

The main reason for having a definite, planned conclusion lies in the importance of establishing the central idea of the sermon in the mind of the listener. A sermon should end with a challenge based upon the theme of the chosen text. If we are expositing the Word, people should know that it is not the preacher but the Lord who is calling for a decision. A well-planned conclusion should awaken a desire to respond to that text. It should arouse enthusiasm for the scriptural theme supported in the message. Too many times people respond intellectually to the Word but never allow the message to affect their emotions and wills. Not every listener will respond, but the goal of reaching the heart of every listener should influence the preacher in the construction of concluding sentences.

It is the nature of the scriptural theme then that determines the nature of the conclusion. Here is another reason why every conclusion will be different. The way you finish a sermon should be just as varied as the themes that prompt you to preach. Buttrick says, "Preaching never talks about things in a flat, detached, nothing-is-at-stake manner. No, the language of preaching, like the language of scripture (much of which is also preaching), is performative; it is a language intending *to do*."[17] The action of the Word must become the action of the sermon. The persuasion of the text must become the persuasive intent of the conclusion. If the text calls for change, we must call for change. If the text evokes wonder, we must promote awe. If the text commands praise, we must expect praise. If the text invites to salvation, we must issue that same invitation.

In many homiletics textbooks the discussion of conclusions centers on the types of materials to be used: quotations, illustrations, poetry, hymns, summary, and so on. Though variety is important in conclusions, those types of materials may be the least effective method of bringing the message to a burning focus in congregational consciousness. At the conclusion of a linear logical sermon, a direct conversation between the preacher and the listener concerning personal responsibility may be the best way to connect the audience to the text. At the end of a narrative sermon, an overheard conversation between two of the characters in the story may have an even greater impact.

The following self-test will concern itself with the effectiveness of the conclusion as it relates to the purpose of the entire message. Use the written transcripts of your sermons along with digital or video recordings to evaluate the variety and impact of your sermon conclusions.

Self-Test for Evaluating Sermon Conclusions

1. Choose at least five different sermons you have preached and recorded. Write down the requested information from each sermon, and

then answer the questions as indicated. You will want to use the transcripts of your sermons for this exercise.

a. Write down the last complete phrase or sentence spoken from the pulpit at the end of these sermons. Exclude any prayers if prayer is a customary way to close after the sermon is complete.

(1) _____

(2) _____

(3) _____

(4) _____

(5) _____

b. Identify the exact place in the sermon where the transition into the conclusion took place, and write that transition sentence on the lines below.

(1) _____

(2) _____

(3) _____

(4) _____

(5) _____

c. Count the number of sentences between the transitional sentence and the final sentence, and write that number below.

(1) _____

(2) _____

(3) _____

(4) _____

(5) _____

d. Classify each conclusion according to the materials or method used. Use the following types of classifications or choose "other" and specify additional methods: summary, return to introduction, quotation, illustration, personal testimony, poetry, action step, question, other.

(1) _____

(2) _____

(3) _____

(4) _____

(5) _____

e. Answer the following questions while considering the information recorded above.

(1) Are any of the classifications in *d* identical?

Yes   No

(2) Is any sentence in *a* a question?

Yes   No

(3) Were there more than 10 sentences in any of the conclusions?

Yes   No

(4) Were there less than 2 sentences in any of the conclusions?

Yes   No

(5) Did you have a hard time determining where the conclusion began in any of the sermons?

Yes   No

(6) Was the transition marked by an identifying phrase such as "in conclusion"?

Yes   No

(7) Did any conclusion contain a reference to time, either in relation to length or brevity of the message?

Yes   No

(8) Did any conclusion seem unrelated to the theme of that sermon?

Yes   No

(9) Did you classify any of the conclusions as "summary"?

Yes   No

(10) Did you classify any of the conclusions as "action step"?

Yes   No

2. Listen carefully to one of your sermon conclusions, and then read the transcript of the same conclusion while considering the answers to the following questions.

a. Does my conclusion introduce new ideas that were not part of the development within the sermon?

Yes   No

b. Does my conclusion review all of the major points of the sermon?

Yes   No

c. Is there an appeal to the audience to do something within this conclusion?

Yes   No

d. Could I recognize the theme of the sermon text simply by hearing the conclusion?

Yes   No

e. Could this conclusion be used for any other sermon I have preached?

    Yes   No

f. Does the sermon wander at the end without coming to a complete stop?

    Yes   No

g. Does the conclusion cause the action of the sermon to extend beyond the closure of the service itself?

    Yes   No

h. Have I used signal words to let the audience know the conclusion is in progress?

    Yes   No

i. Does the conclusion make reference to the sermon introduction?

    Yes   No

j. Can I tell from my final sentence that the sermon is over?

    Yes   No

k. Does my conclusion create a specific image or picture of what obedience to this text will look like?

    Yes   No

l. Does the conclusion speak to the audience in my own voice, rather than in the words of someone else?

    Yes   No

m. Does the conclusion contain a new text of Scripture that has not been part of the previous subject of the message?

    Yes   No

n. Have I included remarks in the conclusion that draw attention to myself rather than to the theme of the sermon?

    Yes   No

o. If I normally extend an invitation after a message, is my conclusion more of a transition into that invitation than it is an ending for the specific sermon topic of the day?

    Yes   No

p. Is my conclusion focused on the future?

    Yes   No

q. Does my conclusion return the listener to the historical past of the Scripture?

    Yes   No

r. Does the conclusion include images that are common to the consciousness of the entire audience?

   Yes   No

s. Are the final sentences of the conclusion designed primarily to affect the emotions of the listener?

   Yes   No

t. Are the final sentences of the conclusion designed primarily to influence the will of the listener?

   Yes   No

SCORING:

1. Starting with 1e, give yourself 1 point for each of the answers listed
   below.

   No. 1—Yes
   No. 2—Yes
   No. 3—Yes
   No. 4—Yes
   No. 5—Yes
   No. 6—Yes
   No. 7—Yes
   No. 8—Yes
   No. 9—Yes
   No. 10—No

2. Give yourself 1 point for each of the following answers.

   a. Yes
   b. Yes
   c. No
   d. No
   e. Yes
   f. Yes
   g. No
   h. Yes
   i. Yes
   j. No
   k. No
   l. No
   m. Yes
   n. Yes

o. Yes

p. No

q. Yes

r. No

s. Yes

t. No

If you scored more than 4 points on this self-test, you would do well to pay close attention to your word choice in the preparation of your conclusions. Use the following exercises to facilitate improvement in the areas of variety, clarity, specificity, simplicity, moving to action, and imagery.

Exercises for the Improvement of Conclusions

1. Each sermon conclusion must be crafted individually to mesh with the goal of the sermon as stated in the biblical theme. For each text and theme in this exercise, list five specific actions that a congregation could be challenged to accomplish in the future as actions of obedience to that text.

   a. Eph. 1:3-14—Theme: Those who have been redeemed should continually praise the Triune God for salvation.

   b. Phil. 4:6-7—Theme: The way we live should reflect the way we pray.

   c. Luke 19:1-10—Theme: We should see the lost world around us through the eyes of Christ.

   d. Prov. 3:1-12—Theme: A God-honoring son should be the desire of every father's heart.

   e. Prov. 31:1-31—Theme: Mothers can protect their daughters from frustration by teaching them to live a life that satisfies.

2. Contrary to popular homiletical opinion, conclusions should not strive for heightened emotional impact or memorable inspirational phraseology. The purpose of preaching is not to get people to remember the message but to get them to obey the message. Choose one of the conclusions from your sermons, and try to rewrite it according to the following guidelines for simplification.

   a. Rewrite every sentence as a simple sentence—one noun and one verb.

   b. Remove any adjectives that occur in tandem.

   c. Make each noun specific rather than general. Say "slinging hamburgers" rather than "your job."

    d. Make each verb active rather than a state of being. Say "shovel the driveway" rather than "be good to your neighbor."

    e. Create imagery that is in the shared consciousness of the listeners. Instead of a phrase like "You may be in a situation this week where you should witness," say, "Sitting in the lunchroom you'll be asked how you handled the death of your mother and you'll share your faith."

    f. Replace abstract words with concrete ones. Change "show love in all your relationships" to "bring flowers when it's not her birthday" or "call that sister you quit talking to a year ago."

3. An effective conclusion will often end quietly and unexpectedly. Think of five ways you could transition to a conclusion without using the words "Finally," "In conclusion," or "Give me five more minutes and I'll be done." Here are a couple of examples: "So we're starting a new millennium." "Maybe you have come to church this morning seeking answers."

4. The following conclusion makes a transition to a standard invitation. Rewrite the conclusion to make it lead to a specific appeal based on the text and biblical theme.

   Text: Phil. 4:6-7

   Theme: The way we live should reflect the way we pray.

   Example: So what did the Lord Jesus Christ do when the bottom had fallen out of His world? He prayed. In the cold night of that terrible week of betrayal, His disciples could have seen their Lord on His knees pouring out His petitions to God, His Father. Here at our church we give an invitation every Sunday for three things: salvation, baptism, and church membership. If you have any of those needs this morning, make your way forward during the hymn of invitation, and someone will meet you at the front to show you from the Word of God how your need can be met.

5. The following conclusion wanders around without ever coming to a complete stop. Rewrite the conclusion in no more than three sentences, focusing it on the specific subject of this text.

   Text: Eph. 1:3-14

   Theme: Those who have been redeemed should continually praise the Triune God for salvation.

   Example: Praise God for everything. He can change every aspect of your life—religious, social, political, home, school, work, and church—and you need to apply this message everywhere on every occasion. Listen up, now. Pay attention. Don't let anything keep you from remembering this. Post it on your mirror; write it in your Bible; and if you don't believe it, you had better get your heart right because if you get your heart right you will believe it. Mark it down. Nothing is more important than praise. "Bless the LORD, O my soul: and all that is within me, bless his holy name" (Ps. 103:1). It will change your life. It changed mine. Isn't there something in your life that needs changing? Praise the Lord. He can change you. Let's pray.

6. The following conclusion creates a specific image or picture of what obedience to this text would look like. Read the text and the conclusion; then use the pattern to rework one of your own conclusions.

   Text: Luke 19:1-10

   Theme: We should see the lost world around us through the eyes of Christ.

   Example: What does it mean to be lost? Albrecht Durer, best known for his sculpture of "Praying Hands," once painted a portrait of the "Prodigal Son." But Durer did not put the prodigal in a pigpen in Palestine. He painted him on a back street of the city of Nuremberg, his own hometown. You may serve a meal to some prodigal in your restaurant this week. You may cut her hair in your beauty salon, change the oil in his car, or brush past him sprawled on the sidewalk in your favorite park. Will we see her? Will we see him the way Christ saw him? Through His eyes? Or through ours?

   a. Your sermon has come to the conclusion, and you want to awaken the minds of your listeners. This conclusion does that with a question. Write a question for each of your sermon conclusions, focusing the attention of the listener on the subject of the sermon.

   b. Choose one of your questions, and develop the paragraph that proceeds from it. Answer the question with specific images of those who exist in the collective consciousness of your congregation.

   c. Try this. Expand the idea of meeting a prodigal in several other places where you know the people in your congregation interact with the lost. Make the image case-specific to your people.

5
Watching Yourself

■ Sermon preparation is a very solitary process. A preacher, alone with the Word of God and the Spirit of God, seeks the mind of God. That search focuses on understanding the text in its grammatical, historical, and literary fullness. You walk alone the paths of the patriarchs and sift privately through the memorabilia of ancient prophets. Even as the process moves from research to organization, the potential audience is present only in the mind of the preacher.

Preaching, on the other hand, is very public. It could be argued that a sermon doesn't really become a sermon until it is preached. As much as some people enjoy reading sermons from the past, there is no real substitute for experiencing a live message. When we present a message live, we clearly use not only our words but also our bodies. Difficulties occur when we plan what our words are going to say but ignore the statements our bodies make. For the teller of the "story," physical communication becomes vastly important. The audience needs to see the scenes and characters in the story as well as hear them. The preacher is not delivering a radio address; this is a live performance.

A communications expert, Mario Pei, "estimated that humans can produce up to 700,000 different physical signs."[1] You may be using many of those signs in the pulpit and unconsciously negating with your body what you are saying with your mouth. Learning to control the body will aid you in coordinating body language with oral language, enhancing the total message instead of detracting from it. "A speaker's body may bring to his speech the whole weight and total force of personality,"[2] add Stevenson and Diehl. When that happens, you will communicate not only with words but with words reinforced and strengthened by your entire being.

For each of the following self-tests you will be using the videotaped or digitally recorded copies of your sermons. Try to watch several sermons, or at least a portion from several, while completing the self-tests, since a repetition or pattern of physical delivery is far more important than isolated instances. A person who stumbles when walking up onto the platform to preach, for example, probably does not have a problem with stumbling. But a person who consistently, week after week, avoids eye contact with his audience does have a problem with that component of effective delivery.

When you determine through a self-test that there is an area where you would like to improve, look at the exercises. Try all of them initially to determine which exercises best fit your situation. Then design a plan of repeated exercise over a period of several weeks until you notice improvement in that area, not just in your exercise time but subconsciously at the time you preach. The exercises should never be the focus of your concentration as you preach. Instead, the good body language habits they instill should become such a part of how you communicate that you automatically incorporate these habits into the preaching experience itself.

GENERAL BODY TENSION

The first great obstacle to the effective use of the body in communication is stress. "The man whose body seems inert in the pulpit may be using up a tremendous amount of physical and nervous energy to inhibit his natural actions,"[3] write Stevenson and Diehl. "He may be holding himself rigid." A physically inhibited speaker seldom realizes that his or her defensive manner is actually communicating something. It is telling people he or she is nervous, warning them to keep their distance, and instructing them to be on their guard because this is going to be an unpleasant experience for everyone. Stress will affect both vocal and physical delivery, so it needs to be considered in the self-evaluation of both.

Test Your Stress Level

Answer the following questions, thinking about which choice fits your situation more closely. There are no right or wrong answers.

1. Do you normally choose your Sunday morning sermon topic
   a. before Tuesday afternoon?
   b. after Thursday morning?

2. When you finish your final sermon on Sunday, are you able to feel relaxed
   a. by the time you arrive back at home?
   b. by the time you have watched the late evening news?

3. Before a service where you are scheduled to preach do you
   a. walk through the auditorium greeting parishioners?
   b. stay in your study so no one can ask questions about church politics?

4. Have you married, added a child to your family, or lost a close family member
   a. no more recent than three years ago?
   b. within the last year?

5. Has your ministry at the present church extended to
   a. two to six years or more?
   b. less than one year?

6. Do your future plans for the next two years include
   a. continuing on in your present position?
   b. preparing for impending retirement?

7. Has your ministry experience in the last year included
   a. increased pastoral involvement in the lives of older saints?
   b. personal involvement in the death of an immediate family member?

8. On the average do the meetings of the official board of your church
   a. last between one and three hours?
   b. extend beyond three hours?

9. Do you plan your preaching schedule
   a. six months to one year in advance?
   b. the week you are expecting to preach?

10. When choosing topics for sermons that need to be addressed in your pulpit,
    a. is your first concern the questions you have been asked by people?
    b. is your first concern the problems you see in the church?

If you checked off *b* more than *a*, you have a tendency toward excess stress that translates into undue tension during preaching. Watch closely tapes of recent sermons while using the "Stress Indicators Analysis."

Stress Indicators Analysis

Instructions: Watch several digital recordings of your sermons with the volume turned off completely. Indicate the best answer to complete each statement.

1. Watch the mouth. Do you see the tongue protruding to wet the lips
   a. during every pause for breathing?
   b. occasionally, every few minutes throughout the sermon?
   c. never (well, maybe once or twice)?

2. Watch the eyes. Do they
   a. focus on one point inside or outside the room and never move?
   b. glance rapidly around the room in constant motion?
   c. focus on the sermon notes with occasional glances at the audience?

3. Watch the hands. Are they
   a. playing with any object such as notes, glasses, tie, keys, Bible, and so forth?
   b. moving in and out of pockets?
   c. obvious only when purposefully used for emphasis?

4. Watch the feet. Do you see someone who is
   a. standing rooted to one spot and not moving at all?
   b. shifting weight back and forth from foot to foot?
   c. standing tall, with weight balanced on both feet?

5. Watch the lips. Do they
   a. often break into a brief smile that never seems to form completely?
   b. purse or press tightly together between words?
   c. move smoothly in a way that does not call attention to themselves?

6. Watch the neck. Does it
   a. seem to be constantly stretching, trying to escape from a tight collar?
   b. remain rigid, allowing head movement only when the entire torso moves?
   c. allow the head to move gracefully when necessary?

7. Watch the stance. Is it best described as
   a. rigid, like a wooden statue?
   b. draped, like a cloth over the pulpit?
   c. poised, like a soldier at ease?

8. Watch the jaw. Does it
   a. seem immobile, making the lips do all the work?

    b. jut out excessively or seem to blend in with the neck?

    c. avoid calling attention to itself by remaining in its normal position?

9. Watch the arms. Is their movement

    a. nonexistent because they are out of sight behind the body?

    b. rapid and repetitious?

    c. what you would expect of a person in normal conversation?

10. Watch the overall bodily movement. Would you describe it as

    a. jerky and mechanical?

    b. stiff and labored?

    c. fluent and uncontrived?

Instructions: Watch the videotaped sermons again, this time with the volume on high, listening carefully to the sound of the sermons.

11. When inhaling are you able to hear the sound of the breath whistling through the teeth?   Yes   No

12. Count the number of breaths taken in one minute. Is breathing more rapid than normal?   Yes   No

13. Is there a noticeable quaver in the voice when compared to conversation during times of rest?   Yes   No

14. Is there a higher average pitch level in the voice when compared to normal conversation?   Yes   No

15. Count the number of verbal fillers ("uh," "um," "OK," etc.) in a five-minute segment of the sermon. Are there more than five?
Yes   No

16. When exhaling, can sounds of escaping breath be heard along with the spoken words?   Yes   No

17. Do you have trouble distinguishing individual words because groups of words sound as if they are all connected?   Yes   No

18. Do you swallow vowel sounds so they appear to be coming from the back of your throat?   Yes   No

19. Is your speech more rapid than normal when compared to your tape of conversation?   Yes   No

20. Does your voice sound strident, jarring, or raspy?   Yes   No

For every answer *a* or *b* in Nos. 1 through 10, give yourself 1 point. For every *yes* in Nos. 11 through 20, give yourself 1 point. If you have 2 or more total points, you are showing some signs of stress. Use the following exercises to design a personal plan for decreasing tension in your delivery.

Exercises for Release of Tension

Every pastor must develop some method of physical and vocal relaxation. Tension, like smiling, is contagious. If you are tense, the people around you will become tense. The goal of relaxation must not be the total elimination of tension, however. Not even pulpits were constructed to support jellyfish. Instead, you must try to get rid of unessential tension in the muscles—that which is not needed in the performance of the preaching task. Relaxation must be selective, conscious, and controlled.

1. Start with the large muscles of the body.
   - Sit. Tense your body. Then relax. Allow your head to fall forward and your arms to dangle loosely at your sides.
   - Rotate your shoulders four or five times—first the right, then the left, then both simultaneously.
   - Lift one leg and stretch it straight, pointing the toe away from the body. After tensing the entire leg, release the tension and let the leg fall. Repeat with the other leg and then with both.
   - Lift one arm in front of you, tensing it and then letting it fall. Repeat with the other arm and then with both.
   - "Pretend that you have accidentally plunged your arm into a barrel of gunk or slime. Shake your arm vigorously to get rid of the repulsive stuff. Repeat, but this time the slime is on your legs, then your torso, and finally the neck and the head."[4]
   - Stretch and begin to yawn. Rather than finishing the yawn, sigh deeply. The stretching part should be intense, but the yawn and sigh should be gentle.

2. Next move on to the smaller muscles, particularly those of the sound-producing mechanism.
   - Stretch your neck forward and downward, tensing your jaw and neck muscles. Let your chin touch your chest. Move your head slowly to your right shoulder, to the rear, to the left shoulder, and forward to the chest again. As you rotate, gradually relax the jaw and neck. Hum deep in your throat.
   - Stand erect and slowly relax at the waist, allowing your entire body to fall forward from the hips while keeping your legs straight. Walk around slowly, like an elephant, with arms dangling loose. Slowly return to the upright position.
   - Reach with one arm as if stretching for a piece of fruit high above your head. When the arm is completely extended, relax the shoulder

and let the arm fall freely. Repeat with the other arm and then with both.

- Keeping your arms limp, twist from the waist, allowing the arms to move freely as you twist.

3. Now relax the lips, tongue, and jaw through vocal exercises.
   - Say the following as though sighing. Stretch the vowel sounds. "Rest in the Lord and wait patiently for him."
   - "Freeze or tense your throat and jaw muscles and then swallow. Holding this extreme tension for a few seconds, say 'ah.' What happens to your vocal quality?"[5]
   - Next, yawn gently as you inhale. Consciously relax your jaw. Can you feel and hear the difference when you say "ah" this time?
   - Open your mouth as widely as you can on the initial sound of each word:

Amram	aloof	aloud	ark
arose	ask	austere	author
obscure	offering	olive	obtain
Omri	ours	hour	owl

4. As a warm-up before speaking, the following exercises should help the body attain the proper degree of tension.
   - Loosen your collar and tie.
   - Hum softly up and down the scale.
   - Sing up and down the scale with an open vowel sound like "oo" or "ah."
   - Sit comfortably and allow the physical tension to escape.
   - Spend time in prayer, focusing your thoughts on the message rather than on the immediate circumstances that may be causing stress.
   - Massage your temples, face, and throat down to your collar line.
   - Press gently on the side of your throat and move your neck back and forth while allowing your hands to massage the neck muscles.
   - Yawn deeply several times trying to keep the relaxed feeling in the throat that occurs when in the middle of the yawn.
   - Allow your head to fall forward and leave it there until you feel the tension in the neck; then bring your head back up slowly while leaving the tension behind.
   - Read slowly and softly a portion from the Psalms, allowing your mind to focus on God and your vocal mechanism to release all remaining unnecessary tension.

- Sit in a relaxed position and deliberately slow your breathing down to no more than four or five times a minute. To do this take as long as possible on a deep inhalation and then exhale as slowly as possible.

FACIAL EXPRESSION

The expression on a person's face can easily negate the message that comes from the mouth. A preacher would have a hard time convincing a listener that "we have known and believed the love that God has for us" (1 John 4:16, NKJV) if hatred were showing on his or her face. "The head and face are the most expressive and impressive parts of the body,"[6] claims Axtell. The face is constantly communicating even when the lips and mouth fall silent. We communicate through nodding or shaking the head, raising the eyebrows, tapping the forehead, scratching, subtle neck movements, glances, opening and closing the mouth, flaring the nostrils, and smiling and frowning. Axtell writes about one Wayne State University researcher who claims, "There are some 1,814,400 different kinds of smiles."[7] In addition to all of those, the eyes are so expressive that they will be considered separately from the rest of the discussion of facial expression.

For the next self-test, turn off the sound on the VCR and watch closely the tape that was made closest to the platform. Then watch the same tape with the sound turned up to normal. During both sessions, concentrate on the movements of the head, nose, lips, tongue, jaw, and neck. The basic question that must be answered is this: Am I communicating the same message with my facial expression as I am communicating with my words?

Self-Test on Facial Expression

1. With the volume off, identify each of the following universal facial expressions during your sermon and record the number indicating the place on the tape where that expression is most evident. If you see no evidence of that facial expression, mark the second column.

	Tape Number	No Evidence
a. Surprise	_____	_____
b. Anger	_____	_____
c. Happiness	_____	_____
d. Fear	_____	_____

e. Disgust   _____   _____
f. Sadness   _____   _____

2. Now with the volume restored, review each of those places where you noted the universal facial expressions and ask yourself if the facial expression agrees with the words you are speaking at that particular time.

   a. Surprise   _____ Agrees   _____ Disagrees
   b. Anger   _____ Agrees   _____ Disagrees
   c. Happiness   _____ Agrees   _____ Disagrees
   d. Fear   _____ Agrees   _____ Disagrees
   e. Disgust   _____ Agrees   _____ Disagrees
   f. Sadness   _____ Agrees   _____ Disagrees

3. With the volume up, watch the tape for places where one of those universal facial expressions would have been appropriate but was not used. Ask yourself if the facial expression you see at those places agrees or disagrees with the message you intended to communicate at that particular time.

   a. Surprise   _____ Agrees   _____ Disagrees
   b. Anger   _____ Agrees   _____ Disagrees
   c. Happiness   _____ Agrees   _____ Disagrees
   d. Fear   _____ Agrees   _____ Disagrees
   e. Disgust   _____ Agrees   _____ Disagrees
   f. Sadness   _____ Agrees   _____ Disagrees

4. With the volume off, count the number of times you smile and frown during the course of a sermon.
   Smiles _____   Frowns _____

5. With the volume on, note the smiles and frowns in relationship to what is being communicated and answer the following questions.

   a. Are my smiles a deliberate reinforcement of positive words?
         Yes   No
   b. Are my smiles a personal response to intended humor?
         Yes   No
   c. Are my smiles a nervous reaction to statements I am not sure are being well received?
         Yes   No
   d. Are my frowns a deliberate reinforcement of negative words?
         Yes   No

    e. Do I use a frown to establish a mood of solemnity or seriousness?
         Yes   No

6. Do my frowns outnumber my smiles?
         Yes   No

7. Does the total number of either smiles or frowns reflect the mood of the topic under discussion in this sermon?
         Yes   No

8. With the volume off, respond to each of the following self-evaluative comments.
    a. I can observe involuntary mouth twitches that don't seem to be consciously controlled.
         Yes   No
    b. I see a neck consistently bent forward rather than remaining erect most of the time.
         Yes   No
    c. I notice an occasional tightening of the jaw or neck muscles between words.
         Yes   No
    d. I see myself emphasizing statements by twisting or jerking my neck and pointing with the jaw.
         Yes   No
    e. I observe a repetitive use of facial expression that loses its effectiveness simply by overuse.
         Yes   No

9. Answer each of the following questions based on your observations and the list of typical facial expressions provided.
    a. What is the typical look my face normally expresses while preaching?
    b. What is the first runner-up for most typical look?
    c. What range of facial expressions do I go through while preaching?
    d. Do my eyebrows move at all? If so, how?
    e. Are there habitual, repetitive changes in any part of my face?
    f. Does my smile come suddenly or slowly and how does it disappear?
    g. Do my facial expressions linger or disappear abruptly?
    h. How is the timing of my facial expressions in relation to my words?

i. Are my facial expressions obvious or somewhat subtle and muted?

j. Would I describe myself as expressive or "poker-faced"?

k. How much energy is present in my facial expression alone?

SCORING: Look back through your answers to the self-test on facial expression. If you conclude that what your face is saying does not always support the message of your words or contradicts that message in any way, you need to work on that aspect of your delivery. Use the following exercises to design a personal plan for improvement in the use of facial expression to enhance communication.

Exercises for Increased Facial Expression

Do the following exercises while watching your face carefully in a mirror.

1. Memorize the following sentence: "I don't understand how you could do this to me." Now say that sentence while allowing your face and voice to communicate the six universal emotions.

   a. Surprise

   b. Anger

   c. Happiness

   d. Fear

   e. Disgust

   f. Sadness

2. Without saying anything, try to re-create each of the facial expressions you identified in the previous exercise. Become familiar with the way your mouth, lips, eyes, forehead, jaw, and neck feel when expressing those emotions.

   a. Surprise

   b. Anger

   c. Happiness

   d. Fear

   e. Disgust

   f. Sadness

3. Read aloud the following passages of Scripture while watching yourself carefully in a mirror. For each passage identify the major emotion called for by the subject matter in the text. Work until you are satisfied that your face is communicating the same emotion as the message of the words.

a. "Whom having not seen you love. Though now you do not see Him, yet believing, you rejoice with joy inexpressible and full of glory" (1 Pet. 1:8, NKJV).
   Emotion? _____

b. "So it was, as soon as he came near the camp, that he saw the calf and the dancing. So Moses' anger became hot, and he cast the tablets out of his hands and broke them at the foot of the mountain" (Exod. 32:19, NKJV).
   Emotion? _____

c. "Now as he reasoned about righteousness, self-control, and the judgment to come, Felix was afraid and answered, 'Go away for now; when I have a convenient time I will call for you'" (Acts 24:25, NKJV).
   Emotion? _____

d. "When she recognized Peter's voice, because of her gladness she did not open the gate, but ran in and announced that Peter stood before the gate" (Acts 12:14, NKJV).
   Emotion? _____

e. "Then they said to her, 'Woman, why are you weeping?' She said to them, 'Because they have taken away my Lord, and I do not know where they have laid Him'" (John 20:13, NKJV).
   Emotion? _____

f. "When Pilate saw that he could not prevail at all, but rather that a tumult was rising, he took water and washed his hands before the multitude, saying, 'I am innocent of the blood of this just Person. You see to it'" (Matt. 27:24, NKJV).
   Emotion? _____

g. "So I said: 'Woe is me, for I am undone! Because I am a man of unclean lips, and I dwell in the midst of a people of unclean lips; for my eyes have seen the King, the LORD of hosts'" (Isa. 6:5, NKJV).
   Emotion? _____

h. "Let them be blotted out of the book of the living, and not be written with the righteous" (Ps. 69:28, NKJV).
   Emotion? _____

4. Transcribe a paragraph from one of your sermons that you identified under No. 3 on the self-test as a place where facial expression would have been appropriate but was not used. Read that paragraph aloud

in front of a mirror until you are satisfied your face is communicating the same message as your voice.

5. Read the following passage, requiring yourself to smile constantly throughout the reading. Repeat, requiring yourself to maintain a constant frown. Then practice using a variety of facial expressions that support the emotions called for in the text.

> When the LORD turned again the captivity of Zion, we were like them that dream. Then was our mouth filled with laughter, and our tongue with singing: then said they among the heathen, The LORD hath done great things for them. The LORD hath done great things for us; whereof we are glad. Turn again our captivity, O LORD, as the streams in the south. They that sow in tears shall reap in joy. He that goeth forth and weepeth, bearing precious seed, shall doubtless come again with rejoicing, bringing his sheaves with him *(Ps. 126:1-6)*.

EYE CONTACT

One of the most effective methods of increasing rapport between a public speaker and his or her audience is the greater use of eye contact. Eye contact with an audience communicates friendliness, interest, and sincerity. So avoiding contact with your listeners through their eyes will tell them you are unfriendly, uninterested, and insincere. Even if that is not true, you will be communicating that message through your eyes. John Hasling in *The Message, the Speaker, the Audience* says, "Looking at an audience does not cause you to be sincere; it is something you do because you are sincere. Unfortunately, however, the sincerity you feel may not be communicated unless you maintain eye contact."[8]

A preacher should always be speaking to people, not focusing on a written text, notes, or the back of the auditorium. "The rule for public speakers is to scan the entire audience, not focusing for too long on or ignoring any one area of the audience,"[9] notes Joseph DeVito. Nothing will draw the attention of listeners more quickly to what you are saying than actually making eye contact with them. Don't look over the tops of their heads or stare into space as if receiving your message from somewhere near the ceiling. It is good to look for friendly, familiar faces, but don't favor any group of individuals or section of the auditorium. Be particularly aware of spatial considerations, or proxemics, when preaching in a room with a balcony. Even preachers with good eye contact often neglect the balcony crowd while speaking.

"Of all facial cues, eye contact is perhaps the single most important one,"[10] concludes Richard Weaver. For that reason an entire section of self-study needs to be devoted to the analysis and development of in-creased eye contact. While taking this self-test, use the recording device placed closest to the platform. Watch the visual recording with the vol-ume turned down, concentrating on the position and use of the eyes. You may also need to use the videotape recorded from a greater distance in order to further evaluate the use of eye contact in relation to the entire audience. Try to watch the tapes while sitting some distance away so that you get a good sense of what people were seeing from various parts of the auditorium.

Self-Test on Eye Contact

1. Watch a sermon with the volume turned down. Have nearby a clock or timepiece with a second hand or digital stopwatch. Record as closely as possible a sequential list of the times when your eyes are looking at the audience and the times when they are looking else-where.

   Example: Eyes up   10 sec.
               Eyes down   08 sec.
               Eyes up   21 sec.
               Eyes down   27 sec.
               Etc.

2. Find a segment on your tape where you read Scripture. Count the number of times you make eye contact with the audience during the reading of a passage.
   Number of times eye contact is made: _____

3. Using the information from No. 1, take 20 instances of eye contact, add the total time of those together, and divide by 20 to get an aver-age. This will show how long your incidents of contact with the audi-ence normally last.
   Average length of eye contact: _____

4. Watch a videotaped sermon without sound and observe carefully the position of the eyes in order to answer the following questions.
   a. Which parts of the audience do you tend to favor with your eye contact?
            The left side
            The right side
            The center

The front
The back
The balcony
None

b. Which parts of the audience do you tend to avoid with eye contact?
The left side
The right side
The center
The front
The back
The balcony
None

c. Where do your eyes tend to focus for long periods of time?
On your notes
On the floor next to the pulpit
On one section of the audience
On the ceiling
On the back wall
None of the above

d. Which of the following best describes your eyes as you see them?
Alert
Interested
Sincere
Blank
Nervous
Friendly
Comatose
Intense

5. Find an illustration from your message or a place where you described what a person was saying, either in direct or indirect discourse. Watch closely the position of the eyes while listening to that portion of the sermon.
a. Did the eyes remain focused on your notes or outline?
Yes   No
b. Did the eyes seem to see the scene being described or the people being addressed in the scene?
Yes   No

    c. Did you gaze into the audience as if they were the ones in the story or the ones talking?

        Yes   No

    d. Did you shift your gaze to a new focus when a new person began to speak within the story?

        Yes   No

    e. Can you see in your eyes the predominant emotion prevalent within the illustration or dialogue portion of the sermon? That is, did your eyes reflect the joy, sorrow, anger, disgust, surprise, or fear of the characters in the story?

        Yes   No

6. Answer each of the following questions based upon your observations.

    a. Are your eyes in contact with the audience far more than in avoidance?

    b. Do those in the back of the auditorium or in the balcony see your eyes more than they do the top of your head?

    c. How intensely would you rate your contact with the audience? 1 to 10, with 10 being the most intense.

    d. Do you scan the entire audience with your eyes while preaching?

    e. Do you favor or avoid any section of the auditorium?

    f. Do you squint or narrow your eyes when you look up from your notes?

    g. Do your eyes open wider when you make eye contact?

    h. Do your eyebrows move at all? If so, how?

    i. Do your eyes communicate friendliness while you are preaching?

    j. Do your eyes communicate sincerity while you are preaching?

    k. Do your eyes communicate interest while you are preaching?

    l. When it is necessary to look away from your audience for whatever reason, how quickly does your contact return?

SCORING: Look back over your observations concerning eye contact. If you have through your analysis identified any of the following patterns of conduct, you need to work on this very important area of improvement in delivery skills.

1. A tendency to avoid eye contact altogether

2. A tendency to avoid certain parts of the audience

3. A tendency to favor certain parts of the audience

4. A tendency to focus on sermon notes or prepared text

5. A tendency toward very short, rapid glances toward the audience

6. A tendency toward absence of emotion in the eyes

7. A tendency toward a cold stare that makes the listener ill at ease

8. A tendency to squint or lower the eyebrows that suggests you are angry

Exercises for Improvement of Eye Contact

Ultimately, eye contact with an audience can be practiced only when you have an audience. The following exercises are designed to make you aware of what you are doing with your eyes so that when you have an audience, eye contact will improve naturally. Throughout these exercises it is important that you "see" people in front of you even if they are not physically present.

1. Ask someone to help you with this exercise. Choose a subject of mutual interest, and carry on a conversation for two minutes, while all of the time avoiding any eye contact. Next, continue the conversation, but force yourself to speak without breaking eye contact or looking away for a period of two minutes. Finally, continue the conversation for another two minutes with normal eye contact.

2. Read the following Scripture passage four times.
   a. During the first reading do not look up at all.
   b. During the second reading look up 2 times.
   c. During the third reading look up 5 times.
   d. During the fourth reading look up 10 times.

   Then Jesus cried out, "When a man believes in me, he does not believe in me only, but in the one who sent me. When he looks at me, he sees the one who sent me. I have come into the world as a light, so that no one who believes in me should stay in darkness. As for the person who hears my words but does not keep them, I do not judge him. For I did not come to judge the world, but to save it. There is a judge for the one who rejects me and does not accept my words; that very word which I spoke will condemn him at the last day. For I did not speak of my own accord, but the Father who sent me commanded me what to say and how to say it. I know that his command leads to eternal life. So whatever I say is just what the Father has told me to say" *(John 12:44-50, NIV).*

3. Go to the auditorium where you normally preach. Scan the room and identify six or seven areas, placing markers of some sort in those areas if necessary. Now read the passage from exercise No. 2 while looking up at the audience six or seven times. Make certain that each time you look up you focus on a different area of the auditorium.

4. Read the passage several times in the auditorium. Each time you read, try to increase the length of time your eyes are focused on the audience rather than on the text. With practice you should be able to decrease the number of times you have to look down at the text and increase the length of time your eyes are in contact with the audience. As the length of eye contact increases, start to scan with your eyes so that two or three areas of the audience are included each time you make eye contact rather than only one.

5. Read the following passage containing direct dialogue by two different voices. Practice focusing your eyes on a different place for each of the two characters. Remember that the focus should be on the same place each time a character speaks, so that your eyes can help your audience see the scene you are creating for them. During this exercise, eye contact should not be with the audience but with the people to whom your characters are speaking within the scene.

> Then he asked Zebah and Zalmunna, "What kind of men did you kill at Tabor?"
>
> "Men like you," they answered, "each one with the bearing of a prince."
>
> Gideon replied, "Those were my brothers, the sons of my own mother. As sure as the LORD lives, if you had spared their lives, I would not kill you." Turning to Jether, his oldest son, he said, "Kill them!" But Jether did not draw his sword, because he was only a boy and was afraid.
>
> Zebah and Zalmunna said, "Come, do it yourself. As is the man, so is his strength." So Gideon stepped forward and killed them, and took the ornaments off their camels' necks (*Judges 8:18-21, NIV*).

GESTURE

Technically "gesture" or "kinesics," as it is often called in speech theory, refers to all of the movement of the body, including facial expression and eye contact. For the sake of convenience, we will use the term in its popular sense to refer to the movements of the arms, torso, and legs during communication.

Gestures are culture-specific according to DeVito. "The meanings that you might assign to any given hand movement will not be the same as those a member of another culture would assign."[11] An understanding of that difference becomes vital for a preacher who addresses a multicultural audience. This preacher will need to know the cultural backgrounds of the various segments of the congregation to be certain his or her gestures are communicating effectively with everyone. On a trip we made to the Philippines with a college group, one of the first instructions given by the missionary concerned proper and improper gestures.

Generally, gestures are divided into five categories: emblems, illustrators, affect displays, regulators, and adaptors. Each of these will be used in the pulpit although in varying degrees.

Emblems are body movements that possess rather specific verbal translations. They are used in place of words. "OK," "Come here," "Go away," "Who, me?" "Be quiet," "I'm tired," "It's cold"—all of these can be shared nonverbally with people of your own culture. One common emblem used in the pulpit is that of bowing the head when it is time to pray. Those who are familiar with the church subculture recognize that as an emblem and assume a position of prayer even when no formal announcement of a coming prayer is made. Those with a nonchurch background may need additional information to make sense of such a signal. We will be safe if we assume visitors have never been to any church. Be certain that emblems communicate with people rather than confuse them.

Illustrators accompany and help translate a verbal message. They make verbal messages more vivid or help clarify what is being said. Each person within a similar culture recognizes the gestures that accompany a message such as "He went that way" or "Come, follow me." Illustrators are natural gestures that should be a part of public communication, provided the preacher is comfortable and at ease. They will be the most common form of gesture used by a preacher. Without illustrators, delivery will appear stiff, but planning them can also make a speaker appear to be insincere, since it seems as if he or she is staging the performance. "A mechanical approach to gestures will produce nothing better than a kind of pulpit or platform puppetry," write Stevenson and Diehl. "The key to living gesture is found not in a special set of directions but in the natural reactions of daily conversation."[12] The goal of using illustrators involves reinforcing words with actions that appear totally natural to your audience. Illustrators must not call attention to themselves but must focus attention on the message.

Affect displays are the movements of the face and body that convey emotional feeling. These are often unconscious but can be intentional as well. Facial expression was discussed in detail in the previous section. Posture and stance are the most common communicators of affect display or emotion when we consider the rest of the body. If a preacher comes to the pulpit in a physical condition of exhaustion, that state will be communicated through posture. But a person may also suggest to an audience that he or she is tired when that is not true, simply because of a poorly aligned body. "When a preacher learns to speak with his whole body, his sermon will be like a printed musical score which is transformed into audible music by a well-conducted symphony orchestra,"[13] say Stevenson and Diehl.

Regulators are movements used to send signals to another speaker. These may include nodding the head to give someone else permission to speak or raising the hand to ask permission to speak. In most sermonic communication those regulators would be unusual because the preacher does not yield to comments from the audience. But audiences do send regulatory signals to the preacher. These could be termed nonverbal feedback. They are signals that will be received by a preacher if he or she remains alert to what is happening in the audience. Regulators could include people looking at their watches, leaning forward in the pew, taking notes, smiling, yawning, nodding agreement, looking puzzled, or sleeping. Public speakers may also use regulators, such as looking at a clock or watch, or closing a Bible or notebook. Be sure that such regulators are communicating accurately. If you close your Bible and still have five minutes of your sermon left, you may lose the attention of those who take their signal from your action instead of your words.

Adaptors are movements that satisfy some unconscious need. They are usually unintentional movements and often go unnoticed. However, when they are noticed, they can quickly become a distraction for an audience. These would include such actions as scratching the head, running hands through hair, biting the lip, licking the lips to relieve dryness, straightening the tie, or adjusting a belt. Such adaptors are usually modified in public and particularly during platform presentations. If they become obvious, they will be almost certain to distract someone, as in the case of the college class that keeps a daily count of how many times the professor pushed his loose glasses back up onto the bridge of his nose. One way to check yourself to see if you are unconsciously using such adaptors would be to watch what one of your junior high boys does when he is asked to mimic the pastor's preaching. Habitual adaptors are usually the source of the most effective mimicry.

Those who attempt to pattern their preaching after someone they admire usually find themselves imitating these unconscious adaptors rather than the elements that made their hero successful. Men who studied under J. Frank Norris, for example, would often imitate his habit of emphatically pulling a long white handkerchief through his clenched fist. But that was not what made his preaching great, and adopting that gesture made only for poor imitation. Others have tried to imitate the explosive physical style of Evangelist Billy Sunday only to find that their movements simply called attention to their actions rather than to the message. Gesture must always be for the purpose of emphasizing the message, so the best gesture is that which is so natural that it remains unnoticed by the audience. The reason we must pay close attention to gesture, however, lies in the parallel truth. The absence of natural gesture calls attention to itself and away from the message in the same way as imitative, overdone, or unnatural gesture does.

While taking the self-test on gesture, watch the sermon recorded further away from the platform so that you can see the movement of the entire body. Watch carefully the actions of the hands and feet as well as posture, stance, and movement about the platform.

Self-Test on Gesture

1. Watch a sermon without sound. Use the tape that was recorded from a distance so that the entire body can be seen. Pay particular attention to the posture assumed by the body. As you watch, respond to the following statements.

   a. Do I lean on the pulpit for support?

   > Yes   No

   b. Do I repeatedly grab the sides of the lectern?

   > Yes   No

   c. Do my shoulders slouch forward so my head is always slightly ahead of my body?

   > Yes   No

    d. Do I stand stiffly as if involved in a military inspection?

         Yes   No

    e. Do I shift my weight back and forth from foot to foot?

         Yes   No

    f. Do I stand comfortably balanced with weight on both feet?

         Yes   No

    g. Do I stand at ease while still maintaining an erect posture?

         Yes   No

    h. Is my head centered above my body as if I am hanging from an invisible string?

         Yes   No

    i. Do I leave my hands free at my sides when not using them for gestures?

         Yes   No

    j. Do I stand away from the pulpit so as not to appear to be connected to it in any way?

         Yes   No

2. Run your recording on fast forward and note any of the following gestures that occur repetitiously. This should be quite obvious while watching yourself in rapid motion.

  _____   *a.*   Pointing at the audience

  _____   *b.*   Slicing movement of the hand

  _____   *c.*   Palms turned upward

  _____   *d.*   Rubbing the chin

  _____   *e.*   Horizontal movement of the hands

  _____   *f.*   Stepping to the right of the pulpit

  _____   *g.*   Stepping to the left of the pulpit

  _____   *h.*   Rubbing the forehead

  _____   *i.*   Folding the hands together in front

  _____   *j.*   Holding the hands together behind your back

  _____   *k.*   Hitching up the waist of your pants

  _____   *l.*   Placing hands into pockets

  _____   *m.* Picking up items such as a pen, paper, or Bible

  _____   *n.*   Adjusting the tie or collar

  _____   *o.*   Other habitual movements

3. Turn the sound back up as you watch the sermon once again. Con-

centrate on the large movements of the body about the platform. As you watch, respond to the following statements.

a. While stationary, how far apart are my feet?

6-8 inches   10-12 inches

b. When I move away from the pulpit, how far do I go?

1-2 steps   More than 2 steps

c. When I leave the pulpit, how quickly do I return to stand behind it?

Less than 10 seconds   More than 10 seconds

d. When I am away from the pulpit, what do I do?

Come to a complete stop   Pace continually

e. What part of my body can be seen most of the time I am preaching?

Only my head   All of my body

f. What direction are most of my movements outside the pulpit?

Toward the audience   Away from the audience

g. How often do I step away from behind the pulpit?

0-2 times per sermon   More than 5 times per sermon

h. Do my movements about the platform help emphasize what I am saying?

Definitely   Not sure

i. What words best describe my platform movement?

Stilted and repetitious   Natural and spontaneous

4. Watch a sermon with the sound on, concentrating on the use of the arms and hands. Since gestures are normally associated with these parts of the body, they deserve special attention from the preacher. Answer the following questions based upon your observations.

a. Do the movements of my hands and arms appear to be planned?

b. Do my gestures coordinate in timing with the words I am trying to emphasize?

c. Are my gestures so large and enthusiastic that they call attention to themselves instead of to the message they support?

d. Are the gestures I use hidden behind the pulpit?

e. Do my arms and hands move constantly or only when necessary for effective emphasis?

f. Do I leave my hands free at my sides when not gesturing?

g. Do I fiddle with anything while preaching, such as keys, eyeglasses, a watch, or a necktie?

h. Do my gestures actually illustrate what I am saying, or do they confuse the audience through their indefiniteness?

i. Do I allow adaptors, such as scratching my head, adjusting my glasses, rubbing my nose, or any other unconscious movement, to detract from my sermon?

j. Do I send visual regulator cues to my audience signaling an end to the sermon when I really have no intention of stopping?

5. Make a video recording of yourself in normal, everyday conversation with someone you know well. Compare that with the visual recording of your preaching while asking yourself the following questions.

a. Do the gestures and movements I use while preaching look similar to those used in normal conversation?

b. Am I more animated or less animated when I preach?

c. Do I use the same gestures in preaching as in conversation?

d. Does my preaching look "natural" in comparison with my conversation?

e. Do I move around more often or less often when I am preaching?

SCORING: For No. 1 on the self-test, give yourself 1 point for every *yes* in *a* through *e* and 1 point for every *no* in *f* through *j*. For No. 2, give yourself 1 point for every item you checked. For No. 3, give yourself 1 point for checking the first answer under *b, c, e, g,* and *i.* Give yourself 1 point for checking the second answer under *a, d, f,* and *h.*

If you received more than 3 points on Nos. 1 to 3 of the self-test, or if your answers to the questions in Nos. 4 or 5 revealed any potential weaknesses with your gestures, plan a program for self-improvement based on the following exercises.

Exercises for Improvement of Gesture

1. Observe yourself in a full-length mirror. Imagine that an invisible wire extends from the top of your head toward the ceiling. Allow that wire to pull you toward the ceiling, aligning your head with your spine. The neck should be free and relaxed; the shoulders spread out, but not back. As you extend toward the ceiling, allow your torso to lengthen and your rib cage to expand. Do not stretch so far that your heels leave the floor, but feel as if your entire body were floating lightly on the balls of the feet.

2. If you identified your problem as a tendency toward stiffness or a lack

of bodily motion, use the following exercises to help you loosen up while speaking. The exercises should be performed with large gestures in order to help you get accustomed to movement while speaking. Remember that during the actual preaching event such movements should be modified so as not to call attention to themselves, but rather to suggest the action of the words.

Read the following sentences out loud, accompanying each of them with the appropriate physical illustrator.

a. "Ho, everyone that thirsteth." (Beckoning with the entire arm)
b. "Depart, go from hence!" (Motioning with both arms)
c. "Watchman, what of the night?" (Cupping the mouth with both hands)
d. "O Absalom, my son, my son." (Raising both hands toward heaven in grief)
e. "And Saul cast the javelin." (Pantomiming the javelin throw)
f. "Woe to the bloody city." (Shaking the clenched fist in judgment)
g. "Who hath believed our report?" (Spreading the arms in question)
h. "Aha, aha." (Pointing an accusatory finger)
i. "I am thy servant." (Deep bow with extended hand)
j. "O that thou wouldest rend the heavens." (Double-clenched fists pleading for action)
k. "Ye have wearied the Lord with your words." (Both hands over the ears)

3. To practice thinking and moving simultaneously, practice the following exercises in accelerating and decelerating. Constant or repetitious movements suggest a static, planned gesture that communicates boredom and lack of creativity. The entire body must be as alive as the voice while a person is preaching.

   a. Extend your arms in front of you and clap at a constant rate of speed. Notice how robotic and static that motion quickly becomes. Next clap at an accelerating rate of speed noting the energy such action generates. Finally clap at an increasingly decelerated rate of speed until the hands seem simply clasped in prayer. Recognize that it is the variety of the motion and not just the motion itself that adds emotional impact to your gesture.

   b. Using the constant, then the accelerating, and finally the decelerating rates of speed, practice each of the following actions. Think about how you can use variety in your gestures while preaching.

(1) Bringing your fist down on the pulpit

(2) Walking from the pulpit to the side of the platform

(3) Turning to look at something behind you

(4) Pointing your finger at someone in the audience

(5) Pointing your finger at an imaginary person on the platform

(6) Walking back and forth across the platform

(7) Sitting in a chair

(8) Lifting your arms above your head (Notice particularly how the different speeds of this action change the message it communicates.)

4. Read the following passage of Scripture aloud. While reading, allow your body to communicate the emotions you would feel if you had just encountered each of the listed experiences. Not all of the experiences will evoke emotions that support the idea of the Scripture passage, but do your best to make your body communicate the emotion rather than the message. After you have tried successfully to communicate all of the emotions through your body language, choose the emotion you feel best communicates the message of the Scripture text and practice reading the verses again with your voice and body in emotional congruence.

a. Emotional experiences to communicate through body language.

(1) You have just received word of the death of both your parents.

(2) You have in hand a letter awarding you a million-dollar settlement in a long-standing insurance case.

(3) Your favorite football team is behind by 6 points in the last seconds of the game and is driving toward the goal line.

(4) Your favorite football team just lost the game on a final second, 45-yard field goal by the opposite team.

(5) You are relaxing in your hammock on a lazy, summer afternoon.

(6) Your wife desperately needs an organ transplant and tests on the closest possible donor have just come back negative, showing the transplant will not work.

(7) You have been hunting and were just ready to pull the trigger and shoot at a moving object in the brush when you realized it was another hunter wearing camouflage instead of blaze orange.

b. Scripture to read with various emotional connotations.

Son of man, set your face toward Jerusalem, preach against the holy places, and prophesy against the land of Israel; and say to the land of Israel, "Thus says the LORD: 'Behold, I am against you, and I will draw My sword out of its sheath and cut off both righteous and wicked from you. Because I will cut off both righteous and wicked from you, therefore My sword shall go out of its sheath against all flesh from south to north, that all flesh may know that I, the LORD, have drawn My sword out of its sheath; it shall not return anymore.'" Sigh therefore, son of man, with a breaking heart, and sigh with bitterness before their eyes. And it shall be when they say to you, "Why are you sighing?" that you shall answer, "Because of the news; when it comes, every heart will melt, all hands will be feeble, every spirit will faint, and all knees will be weak as water. Behold, it is coming and shall be brought to pass," says the Lord GOD *(Ezek. 21:2-7, NKJV)*.

5. Read the following story aloud while walking around on the platform. Use large, exaggerated movements to express the actions within the story. Talk with your hands. Use any movement necessary to help communicate the content of the story. Remember that this exercise is designed to help you feel comfortable with movement. Such large, exaggerated motions will not be appropriate during the actual time of delivery.

Billy had turned and headed for the right field fence as soon as he saw that the ball was going in low. From over his shoulder he watched the ball rise. He knew it was far over his head, but still he ran.

The bleachers, filled beyond capacity, had spilled many of their spectators into the field, and as he ran, Billy shouted, "Stand back!"

With an eye still on the ball, and the crowd parting before him like the Red Sea before Moses, Billy was sure that the ball was going over the fence. So he prayed. It was not a very theological prayer, just something like, "God, if you ever helped a mortal man, help me now to get that ball, and You don't have much time."

Jumping over a bench someone had hauled onto the field, Billy stopped where he thought the ball would come down. But he had guessed short. It was still going over his head. He jumped as high as he could, shoved his left hand out as far as it would go, and felt the thud as the ball hit his glove. The momentum carried him to the ground under a team of horses waiting for their driver, but somehow he held onto the ball.

Tom Johnson, Cleveland, Ohio, at the time, was the first to reach the jubilant Billy.

"Here's a ten, Bill," he cried, stuffing the money into Billy's pocket. "Buy yourself the best hat in Chicago."

Then the other players were on him, pummeling him and cheering him all the way into the clubroom. Finally it quieted down enough for him to get in a word.

"Thanks, fellows. But it wasn't just me out there this afternoon. It wasn't just Billy who caught that ball. It was Billy and God."

And all the men knew that's the way it would be from then on. Billy and God.[14]

6. Stand still and imagine you are scraping your fingernail on a chalk-board. Allow yourself to react the way you would if you heard that noise. Feel the sensations you would feel in your stomach, your feet, your neck, and your fingers.

7. Stand in the pulpit and imagine that you are preaching when you sense that someone has come up and is standing behind you. Feel the emotions you would feel. Ask yourself the questions you would ask: Who is it? Why is he or she there? What does he or she want? Am I in danger? What should I do? Then consider the audience that normally sits in front of you, and try to recall the emotions you feel in their presence. Ask yourself some of the same questions: Who are they? Why are they there? What do they want? What should I do?

8. Choose one of your recent sermons, and practice preaching a section of the sermon without using a pulpit. First, hold your Bible and notes in your hand. Then set them both aside and preach the same section without notes. Be aware of your movements and gestures in both circumstances. Plan one section in an upcoming sermon where you can move away from the pulpit and deliver several minutes of your message directly toward the audience without the pulpit hiding part of you from them.

Along with analyzing, evaluating, and practicing to improve our body language during delivery, we should also examine how we sound while preaching. What do our listeners hear when we speak? Are we using the full extent of our vocal abilities to convey the words of grace God has given us? The next chapter will help us answer these questions and others, as well as show us what we can do to improve in this area.

6
Hearing Yourself

■ Kent plays soccer with two different teams, participating in two and sometimes three games per week. His strength and stamina are excellent, yet he still practices with his soccer buddies every chance he gets. Ron enjoys archery. During hunting season he regularly bags wild turkeys, pheasants, and deer. But during the off-season he practices consistently at the archery range he has set up in his backyard. No hunter would hike 10 miles into the Rocky Mountains and shoot an elk without being certain of having the physical ability to drag the carcass back. Yet many preachers preach week after week with no more vocal exercise than what they get in the actual process of preaching.

The voice is a magnificent instrument given by God. Just as with any other instrument, its effective use demands study, training, and continual practice. As we have observed, most college and seminary preaching courses dwell on the preparation of the content of the sermon. Deane Kemper in *Effective Preaching* notes that this emphasis is proper, since "simply stated, if we are given a choice, skill in sermon preparation is to be preferred to skill in sermon delivery. If the sermon is flawed in content, no amount of vocal facility is going to make it right."[1] However, this appropriate emphasis often leads to inappropriate conclusions. Some seminarians conclude that vocal quality cannot be changed, while others assume that the effort to change is not worth their time.

The choice between content and delivery does not have to be made if a preacher plans his or her time wisely. Good content is basic, and time spent in exegetical study must be a primary focus for the pulpit communicator. But it must not be the only focus. Giving attention to vocal delivery is also important, since "a word wrongly stressed or a sentence wrongly inflected can distort Scripture and that is a serious matter."[2]

According to Lyle Mayer, an expert in the field of voice production, "People who have poor speaking voices—the kind that set your teeth on edge—are almost always unaware of this. We are our most enchanted listeners, and it's human nature for each of us to believe that nobody speaks as well as we do."[3] When we have listened to our own preaching for several years, we become so familiar with the sound of our own voices that we don't really hear what other people hear when we speak. A deliberate attempt must be made to distance ourselves from the immediate sound that is heard not only through the air but also through the bones of our heads. No one else hears us quite the same way we hear ourselves. But we can sit in their place and hear ourselves the way they hear us.

The sound of a preacher's voice may even have an impact far beyond the pulpit. How people hear a person may actually influence their decision to call a pastor in the first place. Mayer cites a college and university study concerning the reasons employers had refused to hire students. "In approximately two-thirds of the cases, the reason given was that the job seeker did not speak effectively during the interview."[4] If people find it difficult to listen to our voices, they will not be likely to look past that and focus intelligently on our ideas.

The purpose for self-evaluation and improvement of vocal variety must be to increase understanding on the part of the audience. Vocal flexibility must not call attention to itself any more than the overt actions of the body. All skills in delivery are for the purpose of enhancing the reception of the message. The preacher's primary goal in improving voice production is the clearer communication of the gospel message. The way to achieve that goal is to be certain that the entire body—physical, mental, and spiritual—is working in unison. If either the body or the voice is communicating a different message than the mind, the impact upon the listener will be sharply curtailed.

What kind of a voice will enhance rather than diminish that impact? Think about the voices of news or sports commentators, talk-show hostesses, preachers, or politicians you enjoy hearing. They all share a quality that could be described as pleasing. Other voices on radio or television may irritate you. In each case you are hearing the speaker's vocal signature. Vocal quality is what makes a voice recognizable over the telephone or when coming from the next room. It is essentially a result of personality, but in some cases quality can be misleading. Because of undesirable vocal qualities, some people are thought to be arrogant, irritable, withdrawn, sarcastic, or mean when they are not that way at all. It would be a shame if such undesirable vocal qualities convinced a person to shut out a message from God because of the voice of the preacher.

That doesn't have to happen. Without losing your vocal signature, you can develop a pleasing quality in your voice by eliminating its undesirable aspects.

The voice that impacts listeners will also be characterized by clarity of articulation. It will produce distinct sounds that are intelligible and easy to understand. Because preachers talk publicly so often, they can easily fall into habits of indistinct speech. When made aware of their lack of clarity, many try to cure it by being overprecise, which also calls attention to itself and away from the message. "The good voice is easily intelligible without being conspicuously so,"[5] says Anderson. A pleasing voice will be understood without great effort on the part of the listener and without seeming effort on the part of the speaker.

Effective communicators also speak with adequate loudness. There is a tendency to depend on mechanical methods for volume control in this day of lapel microphones and jumbo sound systems. Few modern preachers will ever be faced with the awesome task of preaching to crowds of thousands in the open air like John Wesley or George Whitefield. But even a modern preacher with a lapel mic needs to be certain he or she is speaking loud enough for everyone in the audience to hear. The use of amplification devices can actually work against a speaker. Attempts to emphasize a point by means of volume can result in extreme discomfort on the part of those sitting near the speakers. Decreasing volume for emphasis may result in a total loss of communication if the preacher depends on the amplification system alone to project his voice. Adequate volume also communicates an aura of confidence to an audience. "A voice that is excessively faint or frail annoys most people. It also labels you as timid and weak-kneed,"[6] according to Mayer. A voice that people don't have to strain to hear suggests assurance and conviction.

Analyzing the voices of those you enjoy hearing will also demonstrate the importance of effective pitch level. One reason no absolute rules can be legislated for effectiveness in this area of vocal control is that the best pitch level differs from person to person and from situation to situation. However, it is usually very easy to determine when improper pitch levels are being used. A preacher should not sound like a circus barker, but neither should he or she sound like a Shakespearean actor. Every speaker must determine what basic pitch level is the most suitable, both personally and situationally. Don't try to sound like anyone else. After the optimum pitch level is determined, the flexible voice will use a variety of pitch levels to effectively communicate the emotional inflections of the ideas being presented.

Flexibility or variety is an important component of any speaker's vocal expression. As mentioned in chapter 3, only four things can really be changed about the voice: volume, pitch, rate, and quality. Almost all communication arises as a result of the interaction of these four. We express ourselves through our capacity to vary these four aspects. For example, variety in volume is more important than being loud or soft once we have established that we can be adequately heard. By varying our volume we express excitement, fear, anger, pity, reverence, awe, pride, dominance, and weakness. Weaver defines the concept in this fashion. "Vocal cues are what is lost when your words are written down. The term often used to refer to this quality is paralanguage."[7] Paralanguage includes all of the sounds you make while speaking other than the words themselves. It would include pace, pitch, volume, and all other nonverbal vocal cues.

Variety in pacing, or rate of speaking, is more important than whether we speak quickly or slowly overall. It is possible to have such a rapid pacing that words become muddled and unintelligible. It is also possible to speak so slowly that an audience loses the ability to remain focused on the message. But once we have faced the problems associated with articulation and basic energy, we can use variety in pacing to greatly enhance the effectiveness of communication. There are passages in Scripture that just plead to be read with a more rapid pace. "Make haste, O God, to deliver me; make haste to help me, O LORD" (Ps. 70:1) would lose all its energy if read at a plodding pace. Throughout the course of a message emotions will change. A voice that an audience finds pleasing will vary the rate of speed in accordance with those emotional changes.

One of the most effective methods of emphasis available to the preacher is the pause. This is also related to variety in pacing. A thought-filled silence will allow an audience to reflect on what has just been said. It will also let them anticipate what is yet to come. With this awesome tool of silence available to them, it is unfortunate that too many preachers fail to put it to use. Instead, they inflate every pause with verbal fillers such as "uh," "um," "OK," and "Amen."

Variety of pitch level is probably the most effective method available to a communicator for the transmission of precise differences in meaning. You can take a one-syllable sound like "Oh" and make it take on a great variety of meanings simply by varying the pitch, inflection, or intonation of that syllable. It could mean anything from "I'm really interested" to "That is the most disgusting idea I have ever heard." Changing the pitch of one word at the very end of a sentence can mean the difference between a statement of fact and a question. So variety in pitch is more important than whether you have a baritone or an alto voice.

Variety in quality is also extremely useful to the preacher. Once you have eliminated those irritating qualities that detract from vocal tone, you can work on developing a voice that is so in tune with your emotional state that an audience can tell from the changes in vocal quality what you are feeling. The key to variety in quality of the voice lies in the responsiveness of the speaker to the material. When a preacher is passionately consumed by a message, the body tension will adjust to the meaning being expressed and the appropriate quality in the voice will be the result. For example, think about what happens to a voice when emotion causes a person to fight back tears. That emotion cannot be hidden by the voice. The desire to develop a more expressive vocal variety must never be thought of as a means of producing false or acted emotion. Instead, by improving the ability of our voice to communicate throughout a full range of pitch, volume, pacing, and quality, we make it possible for the voice, along with gestures and words, to effectively communicate the glorious truth of the Word of God. That expressiveness cannot help but impact body, soul, and spirit.

For each of the following self-tests, you will be using the audio as well as the visual recordings of your sermons. Try to watch and listen to several sermons, or at least a portion from several, while completing the self-tests, since a repetition or pattern of vocal variety is far more important than isolated instances of verbal stumbling. Saying "Paul" when you mean "Peter" will probably not mislead anyone during a sermon from the Gospels. But consistently dropping a sound from Philippians so that it comes out as "Flipians" may keep some people from ever figuring out what you are really saying.

When you determine by means of a self-test that there is an area where you would like to improve, look at the exercises. Try all of them initially to determine which exercises best fit your situation. Then design a plan of repeated exercise over a period of several weeks until you notice improvement in that area, not just in your exercise time but subconsciously at the time you preach. The exercises should never be the focus of your concentration as you preach. Instead they should become such a part of the communication experience that you incorporate good verbal language habits into the preaching experience itself.

BREATHING

The primary purpose for breathing has nothing to do with vocal communication. The basic reason for breathing is to sustain life. Since we have been breathing since birth, we give the process little thought, but breathing is one of our strongest biological drives. Oxygen cannot be stored in the body, so it must be continually renewed. "A few minutes without this vital substance, and the tissues of the body begin to break down, the higher levels of the nervous system being the first to suffer,"[8] says Anderson. This dependence on a constant oxygen supply means that we must make some conscious adjustments when breathing to speak.

The greatest difference between breathing to speak and breathing to sustain life involves the length of inhalation and exhalation. During normal breathing the intake and release of breath take about the same length of time. When breathing for speech, however, inhalation becomes very rapid and exhalation may be extended five or six times the length of the intake. There are other differences as well. In breathing to live, exhalation is passive. The diaphragm plays an unconscious part. Breathing for speech requires an active process of exhalation. We must be aware of the work of the diaphragm and consciously control the muscles that parcel out the air needed to support the tone. Breathing to live calls for inhalation that is comparatively shallow, while breathing to speak involves a fuller and deeper intake of air. Stevenson and Diehl remind us that "since we cannot ordinarily inhale while actually emitting tone, during speech we have to inhale quickly in the pauses between phrases."[9]

If a person is not careful, he or she can develop a habit of taking too shallow a breath during those pauses and as a result not have enough air to support the tone that follows. This can affect both loudness and tone quality. Lack of breath support will keep you from speaking with force. It will also make you strain to croak out the last few syllables of a phrase containing one complete thought.

Some people also develop the habit of inhaling too deeply while speaking, a problem that produces breathiness and the irritating release of unused air, often in connection with such sounds as *s* and *c*.

The solution to problems with breath control is not simply learning to breathe with the diaphragm, although many books have suggested that as an answer. (Actually no one breathes without using the diaphragm.) The solution to these problems lies in learning to consciously control the inhalation-exhalation process so that your body always has the appropriate amount of air to support your tone.

While taking the following self-tests, try to listen to several sermons, paying particular attention to the vocal sounds. To help you concentrate on the specific sounds, you may want to alternate between the use of the audio and video recordings. Turn them up almost to an uncomfortable level so that you cannot ignore any of the sounds being produced by your voice. Try to listen to yourself as if you were a stranger. Don't ignore extra sounds that really did come from your throat, and don't allow your mind to fill in syllables or sounds that seem to be missing on the tape. Remember, you want to improve the way others are hearing your voice, not to defend what you are doing because you find it comfortable and familiar.

Self-Test for Breath Control

1. Watch yourself closely on videotape. Take particular notice of the actions of the torso from the waist to the neck. As you watch, respond to the following statements.

   a. Do I ever raise my shoulders while inhaling?

       Yes   No

   b. Do I ever hunch my shoulders forward just before taking a new breath?

       Yes   No

   c. Do I ever visually draw my shoulders back when inhaling?

       Yes   No

   d. Does my neck tighten when I arrive at the end of a spoken phrase?

       Yes   No

2. Listen to a 10- to 12-minute portion of a sermon, timing the intervals between breathing. Write down the length of time it takes you to breathe, and then record the length of time you speak following each breath.

	Time in Seconds
Inhalation	_____
Exhalation	_____

Inhalation   _____

Exhalation   _____

(Etc.)

   a. What is the approximate ratio of inhalation to exhalation while speaking?

       1:3   1:6   1:9

   b. What is the approximate interval between breaths?

       6 seconds   10 seconds   20 seconds

   c. Which word best describes my pattern of inhalation and exhalation?

       Varied   Regular   Choppy

3. Listen closely to the phrasing of your thoughts when preaching several sermons. For this self-test use the audiotapes.

   a. Am I always able to complete a thought before pausing to breathe?

       Yes   No

   b. Do I often release extra air after completing a phrase?

       Yes   No

   c. Can I hear a vocal intake of breath when I inhale?

       Yes   No

   d. Do I often release air at the beginning of a phrase before actually making any speech sounds?

       Yes   No

   e. Do I ever allow air to escape between words and phrases, even though I am not taking a breath?

       Yes   No

   f. Do I sometimes stop in the middle of a phrase to catch a quick breath?

       Yes   No

   g. Do I sometimes sound as if I am straining to complete a phrase without adequate breath support?

       Yes   No

   h. Do I ever hear a gasp for breath when I stop to breathe?

       Yes   No

   i. Do I hear any clicking, popping, or hissing sounds when I inhale?

       Yes   No

   j. Do I hear any clicking, popping, or hissing sounds when I exhale?

       Yes   No

   k. Do I hear any breath leaks on sounds such as "s," "sh," "th," and "f"?
      Yes   No
   l. Do I always inhale silently and unobtrusively?
      Yes   No

SCORING: Give yourself 1 point for every *Yes* in No. 1. In No. 2 the following answers should earn 1 point each: *(a)* "1:3"; *(b)* "6 seconds"; *(c)* "choppy." Give yourself 1 point for every *no* answer to *a* and *l,* in No. 3; and every *yes* answer to *b, c, d, e, f, g, h, i, j,* and *k,* in No. 3. If your total score equals 3 or more, consider which of the following exercises will be the most helpful in controlling your breathing while preaching.

Exercises for Breath Control

Control of Inhalation

1. Check your posture. Stand with your back against a wall, trying to touch the wall all the way from heels to head. Is it difficult to touch the back of your head to the wall in this position? One good device for aligning your body frame properly is to pretend that someone is pulling you up from above like a puppet, with a string tied to the top of your ears (not your nose). Try speaking with this posture and see if your control of breathing is easier.

2. Inhale quickly. Ideally, the listener should not even be aware that the speaker is breathing. Inhale through the mouth during speech. While inhaling, try the two methods of breathing, exaggerating the movements involved.

   a. Raise the shoulders and collarbone while inhaling. Push the shoulders back as you take in the air and then slouch and compress the chest area as you exhale.

   b. Now place your hands just below the rib cage and exaggerate the motion of the diaphragmatic muscle as you inhale and exhale. It is this method of breathing that should seem more natural.

3. If you have a tendency toward shoulder or collarbone movements while speaking, practice the following exercises.

   a. Place your hands on your chest just below the shoulders. Count loudly from 1 to 10. If there is excessive motion of the upper chest, repeat the exercise using your hands to keep that part of the body motionless. Awareness of the movement will be the first step toward its control.

    b. Stand comfortably beside a desk or other heavy object at about the level of your hands. Grab the underside of the desk. In this position your shoulders should not be able to rise. Inhale deeply, concentrating on the movement of the diaphragm.

    c. Hold a book against your stomach just below the area of the ribs. Inhale. The book should move an inch or more. Then exhale and notice how the contraction allows the book to go back in. Continue breathing to become familiar with the feel of that action.

4. Avoid overbreathing. It is better to breathe more frequently than to try to fill up your lungs for a long, interminable exhalation. Inhaling too deeply is often followed by a sigh or other sound before speech resumes, or by very breathy speech.

    a. Read the following selection, pausing at each slash mark (/) to breathe. Avoid taking in too much air. Instead inhale only the amount of air you will need to adequately support the next phrase.

> In the third year of the reign of Jehoiakim king of Judah / came Nebuchadnezzar king of Babylon unto Jerusalem, and besieged it. / And the Lord gave Jehoiakim king of Judah into his hand, with part of the vessels of the house of God: / which he carried into the land of Shinar to the house of his god; / and he brought the vessels into the treasure house of his god / (Dan. 1:1-2).

    b. Reread the same selection, but this time take a deep breath at every slash mark (/). Notice how quickly the lungs fill up with unused air. You will probably find that unintentional release of that unused air also occurs.

Control of Exhalation

1. Effective breathing for speech involves learning to exhale economically. Practice spending your breath wisely. Counting aloud is an excellent exercise for improving your control. Inhale lightly and count with moderate force: 1-2-3-4-5. Inhale and count: 1-2-3-4-5-6-7-8-9. Inhale and count: 1-2-3-4-5-6-7-8-9-10-11-12-13. You should not feel out of breath at the end.

2. Effective breathing also involves learning to prevent fading of vocal intensity. If the last few words of many of your sentences cannot be

heard, though they begin loudly enough, your problem is one of fading. To prevent fading, exhalation must be controlled to the very end of the sentence by means of the gradual and conscious relaxation of the diaphragm.

Read the following psalms, each on a single breath. The first ones will be easy. As the selections become longer, work diligently to conserve your breath, avoiding any unnecessary release of air.

- "Save me, O God; for the waters are come in unto my soul" (Ps. 69:1).
- "LORD, how are they increased that trouble me! many are they that rise up against me" (Ps. 3:1).
- "And now shall mine head be lifted up above mine enemies round about me: therefore will I offer in his tabernacle sacrifices of joy; I will sing, yea, I will sing praises unto the LORD" (Ps. 27:6).
- "A good man sheweth favour, and lendeth: he will guide his affairs with discretion. Surely he shall not be moved for ever: the righteous shall be in everlasting remembrance. He shall not be afraid of evil tidings: his heart is fixed, trusting in the LORD" (Ps. 112:5-7).
- "How amiable are thy tabernacles, O LORD of hosts! My soul longeth, yea, even fainteth for the courts of the LORD: my heart and my flesh crieth out for the living God. Yea, the sparrow hath found an house, and the swallow a nest for herself, where she may lay her young, even thine altars, O LORD of hosts, my King, and my God. Blessed are they that dwell in thy house: they will be still praising thee" (Ps. 84:1-4).

3. To help you relax and develop sensitivity while increasing your ability to sustain sound on one breath, flutter your lips by blowing air through them (like a child imitating a racing car). Time your efforts and seek to increase the amount of time you can sustain an even and regular sound without starts and stops.

4. Gently release the air from your lungs. As it flows out, it should sound like a soft, effortless *fffffffffffffff*. Be sure you are making a sound, and try to increase the amount of time that sound can be sustained without fading. Try the same exercise with the "s" sound.

5. Sigh three times: a small, relaxed sigh; a medium, happy sigh; a huge sigh of relief (you expected a $1,500 bill from the dentist, and instead insurance paid it all). Now yawn and walk around the room, breathing

deeply and sighing. Swing your arms freely and all of the time keep your mouth open and your throat relaxed in the yawning position.

6. Try the following experiment: Hold a small candle about six to eight inches in front of your mouth. Sustain "s" and then try "f." Keep your exhalation regular and constant. The flame shouldn't flicker and certainly shouldn't go out.

7. Count aloud in a march rhythm, voicing the first three beats and resting on the fourth: 1, 2, 3, __; 1, 2, 3, __; 1, 2, 3, __; 1, 2, 3, __; 1, 2, 3, __; 1, 2, 3, __. Do this all on one breath, being sure to maintain a rest that is the same length as the other beats. Do not inhale or exhale during the rests and do not allow extra air to escape while you are resting.

8. Repeat the sound "hah" on one breath several times. Sustain each "hah" for two seconds, pausing for two seconds between each "hah." Do not inhale or exhale during the pauses. Be careful not to allow any breath to escape except when you are actually voicing the "hah."

RESONANCE

Remember your first stereo system? You were probably satisfied with two small speakers on a portable boom box. But that satisfaction did not last for long. From there you added woofers and tweeters, quadraphonic speakers, and surround sound in an effort to obtain the best possible sound from your cassettes and compact discs. Resonance, or enrichment of sound in the voice, is similar to what is happening when you add speakers to your stereo system. As Mayer describes it, "Different parts of the original tone are emphasized or built up, and other parts are damped or filtered out."[10]

Nearly every preacher needs to improve resonance, simply because a preacher uses his or her voice to a far greater degree than most other professionals. Like actors, a preacher calls upon his or her vocal mechanism continuously for long periods of time, often several times a week. Through proper resonance, a preacher can increase volume and vocal power without straining and damaging the unique physical mechanism given by God. Robert Cohen says, "Resonance is a way of making your cavities work for you rather than against you—and is therefore a vocal asset that must be carefully cultivated."[11]

Resonance begins with the movement of the vocal folds. When you are speaking, these two muscles vibrate incredibly fast. When humming, for example, the vocal folds may be vibrating at 256 cycles per second. This vibration produces a sound that must then be reinforced, enriched, and modified by the resonators. The human body has several resonators, including the throat; the nasal cavities; the mouth; and, to a lesser degree, the chest. Improper use of any or all of these resonators will cause vocal stress and result in poor vocal quality at best and physical harm to the speaking mechanism at worst.

Posture provides the key to the proper functioning of the throat as a resonator. The larynx, which contains the vocal folds, is most easily detected by its forward knob, commonly called the "Adam's apple." When you swallow, you can feel the Adam's apple rise in the throat. When speaking, you want to find a posture that will allow the larynx to drop as low as possible in the throat. This will lengthen the column of air in the throat above the vocal folds and provide a greater area for possible reinforcement of the tone. Mayer says that "openness of throat, relative relaxation of the constrictor muscles, walls, and surfaces will emphasize and give prominence to the fundamental and lower overtones and damp out some of the higher overtones and frequencies. The resulting vocal quality may be relatively mellow, full, and rich."[12]

The mouth provides the most versatile cavity for modification and amplification of vocal resonance. The roof of the mouth reflects sound, while the tongue, lips, and inner surfaces of the cheeks absorb it. The possible formations of the teeth, lips, jaw, tongue, and hard palate give the speaker an almost limitless number of combinations for the production and amplification of sound. The vowel sounds in particular are dependent upon the mouth cavity for their resonance. The key to proper resonance from the vocal cavity issues from a relaxed, open-jaw, open-mouth articulation. The more responsive the teeth, tongue, lips, and jaw are to the control of the communicator, the more resonant will be the resulting voice. Tension and immobility in any of those parts of the mouth will decrease the amplitude of resonance.

The nasal cavity is primarily responsible for only the "m," "n," and "ng" sounds. It may also have a damping or softening effect on other sounds resonated by the throat and mouth.

Self-Test for Exploring Resonance

1. Listen closely to a sermon while watching the videotape filmed clos-

est to the platform. Pay particular attention to the quality of the voice you are hearing. Try to listen to yourself as if you were listening to a stranger.

a. Do any of your words sound as if they are being half-whispered?

Yes No

b. Do you hear any audible inhalation, such as a gulp for breath?

Yes No

c. Are any phrases interrupted by breath in a way that seems inappropriate?

Yes No

d. Does your voice sound the same throughout with little variety?

Yes No

e. Is the general impression one of a lack of vocal energy?

Yes No

f. Are you hearing an escape of air that is not part of the words you are saying?

Yes No

g. Do you sound as if you are out of breath from running?

Yes No

2. Answer the following questions while listening to a videotape. Turn the volume up so you can concentrate on hearing all of the paralanguage sounds recorded on the tape. At the same time notice the area of the throat.

a. Do the muscles of the neck seem to knot or bulge while you are speaking?

Yes No

b. Do you sound as if you have just been cheering your favorite team to a double-overtime victory, especially toward the end of the sermon?

Yes No

c. Does your voice sound significantly lower in pitch than when you speak in normal conversation?

Yes No

d. Does your voice seem significantly higher in pitch than when you speak in normal conversation?

Yes No

e. Do your consonants sound hard or rough, especially at the beginning and end of words?

    Yes   No

f. Does your overall tone quality seem unsympathetic and cold?

    Yes   No

g. Do you speak for long periods of time without smiling or looking pleasant?

    Yes   No

h. Do you hear in your voice a tendency to be overbearing and aggressive?

    Yes   No

i. Do some of your words take on a screeching sound, as if they are being squeezed out of your throat?

    Yes   No

3. Listen only to the audiotape while taking this portion of the self-test. Concentrate on the sound of your speaking voice in comparison to the sound of your voice in normal conversation.

a. Do you sound as if you constantly need to clear your throat?

    Yes   No

b. Do you sound as if you have a slight cold when you really don't?

    Yes   No

c. Does your voice sound significantly lower than in normal conversation?

    Yes   No

d. Do your vowels sound as if they are originating in the back of your throat instead of in the front of the mouth?

    Yes   No

e. Are you trying to deliberately lower your pitch in imitation of a speaker whose voice you admire?

    Yes   No

f. Could your sound be described as "smoker's voice" even though you don't smoke?

    Yes   No

4. Once again listen closely to yourself on audiotape. Listen for words that include the "m," "n," and "ng" sounds. Play those portions of the sermon over several times, concentrating carefully on how you are forming those three sounds.

a. Do you sound as if your nose is congested when it is not?

    Yes   No

b. Does your voice sound stuffy when you use "m," "n," and "ng"?

    Yes   No

c. Does "m" sound like "b," "n" sound like "d," or "ng" sound like "g"?

    Yes   No

d. Do you hear a snort of air coming from the nose when you say words with initial "k," "p," or "f" sounds?

    Yes   No

e. Does your voice have a twang worthy of a country-and-western singer?

    Yes   No

f. Do your vowel sounds seem to be coming through the nose when they occur next to "m," "n," or "ng"?

    Yes   No

5. Take this self-test without dependence on any tape. Hum "m" for a few seconds, and then pinch your nostrils with your thumb and forefinger. You will cut off the sounds. Next sing "ah," and once again pinch your nose. It should not affect the sound at all. Finally force yourself to sing "ah" through your nose and pinch the nostrils. Once again the sound will be cut off. Remember that only "m," "n," and "ng" should require nasal resonance.

6. Watch a videotaped sermon, listening closely to your voice while responding to the following statements.

a. Does your voice sound as if it is coming from the bottom of a barrel?

    Yes   No

b. Do your vowel sounds seem hollow or heavy?

    Yes   No

c. Can you see obvious lip movement while you are speaking?

    Yes   No

d. Can you ever see your teeth while you are speaking?

    Yes   No

e. Do you sound as if you are talking with food in your mouth?

    Yes   No

f. Do you keep your chin back against your neck while speaking?

    Yes   No

7. For this test, use the audiotape. Try not to listen to the words themselves, but instead listen for sounds that occur between words, or at the beginning and end of sentences.

   a. Do your lips ever smack together producing a sound like the "putt" of a boat engine?

         Yes   No

   b. Does the end of any sentence drop so rapidly in pitch that a croaking sound occurs?

         Yes   No

   c. Do the last few words of any sentences sound rushed, like the popping of popcorn?

         Yes   No

   d. Are there sounds on the tape you cannot identify although they obviously came from your mouth?

         Yes   No

   e. Do you often find it impossible to hear clearly the last sound of a sentence?

         Yes   No

SCORING: If you answered *yes* to any of the statements in No. 1, you may have a problem with breathiness.

If you answered *yes* to any of the statements in No. 2, you may have a problem with harshness or stridency.

If you answered *yes* to any of the statements in No. 3, you may have a problem with hoarseness.

If you answered *yes* to any of the statements in No. 4 *a, b,* or *c,* you may have a problem with denasality.

If you answered *yes* to any of the statements in No. 4 *d, e,* or *f,* you have a problem with nasality.

If you answered *yes* to any of the statements in No. 6, you may have a problem with throatiness or a muffled tone.

If you answered *yes* to any of the statements in No. 7, you may have a problem with vocal fry.

Exercises for Improving Resonance

NOTE: If you have a chronic problem with any of the above and normally experience vocal strain, excessive hoarseness, chronic laryngitis, or physical discomfort in the vocal mechanism after preaching, seek the advice and care of a physician. Speaking continually with undue tension in the throat can cause severe medical problems. The exercises are designed to help remedy those conditions that produce an irritating vocal quality even though problems are not at the level of demanding serious medical attention.

Exercises for Awareness of Resonance

1. Say the nonsense syllables "bah," "dah," "fah," "kah," "tah" while standing erect and swinging your arms from side to side. Repeat while tipping your head forward until your chin touches your neck. Repeat while swallowing and forming the sounds deep in the throat. Repeat while sending air out though your nose.

2. Place your hands on your cheeks and repeat "oo ah oo ah oo ah" and then "oo eh oo eh oo eh." Notice the vibration in the cheeks on the "oo" sound that is formed in the back of the mouth and requires cheek resonance.

3. Rest a finger lightly on the top of the nose and notice the vibrations when saying "bah bin bah bin bah bin." The nasal consonant combined with "i" should create more nasal resonance than "bah."

Exercises for Relaxation of the Resonators

1. Tense your throat muscles and swallow. Holding that position of the throat, say, "Ah, the love of God." Listen closely to the effect on your vocal quality.

2. Yawn deeply, relaxing the jaw, and repeat, "Ah, the love of God." Notice the contrast in quality with the previous exercise.

3. Maintaining the same open throat as in No. 2, say the following words:

pray	Paul	law	laud
home	how	claw	clave
saw	say	town	ten

4. Force yourself to open your mouth in an exaggerated fashion as you expand the vowels in the following statements. Read each sentence with an open throat.
   a. Thou art fair, my love.
   b. She anointed the body with oil.
   c. From sea to shining sea.
   d. Oh, for a thousand tongues to sing.
   e. "My God, my God, why hast thou forsaken me?" (Ps. 22:1).

f. Come to my heart, Lord Jesus.

g. Over and over and over again.

h. Miriam murmured against Moses.

5. With a relaxed and open throat, try chanting one of the psalms. Alternate between chanting and reading normally verse-by-verse. Each time you read normally, work to bring more of the resonance of the chant into your normal speech without allowing your speech to sound affected.

Exercises to Eliminate Breathiness

1. To eliminate the release of extra air while speaking, a person must hear the sound of his or her voice without the breathiness and remember the muscle tension that was necessary to control the column of air. You must monitor your own voice. The following exercises are designed to help you study the tension necessary to achieve control and make that tension habitual so that it occurs unconsciously while preaching.

   a. Vertical pushups. Do pushups from a standing position, placing your hands on the wall an arm's length away. During the movement of the pushup toward the wall, say "Oh" for several repetitions. Then say "Oh" on several repetitions while your arms are pushing you away from the wall. Feel the increase and release of tension in your shoulders and neck muscles, and listen to when your voice has the most firmness and clarity of tone.

   b. Free weights. Hold a set of barbells or two heavy books out to either side, keeping your arms extended at shoulder height. While maintaining this position, count aloud from 50 to 60. Repeat the exercise, each time concentrating on maintaining clarity of vocal tone.

   c. Raise the desk. Sit comfortably with your knees under your desk. Place your hands under the desk, palms up, and push up on the desk as if to raise it with only your arms. While pushing count aloud from 50 to 60. Notice the tension in the arms and the neck, and evaluate the effect of that tension on tone quality and the elimination of breathiness.

   d. Samson's Gaza gates. Stand in an open doorway and press your palms against the sides of the door for several seconds. Release the pressure, and count firmly from 50 to 60. The larynx should retain tension from the action of the hands against the door.

2. Often breathiness is word or sound specific. It occurs only on certain troublesome consonants at the beginning and ending of words. Repeat aloud the following list of words, carefully conserving your breath and consciously cutting short the time you spend on the voiceless consonants.

son	shine	sunshine	folds
sheep	boys	sheepfolds	tents
sling	shot	slingshots	wish
sing	psalm	psalms	weapon
sword	when	missed	holy

3. Read the list of words again. This time almost completely eliminate the sounds that have been underlined. Cut them as short as possible.

son	shine	sunshine	folds
sheep	boys	sheepfolds	tents
sling	shot	slingshots	wish
sing	psalm	psalms	weapon
sword	when	missed	holy

4. Read the following sentences beginning with a very low volume and gradually increasing the volume until breathiness is eliminated. Lack of adequate volume is often one of the reasons for a breathy tone.

   a. I can say that the joy of the Lord has certainly strengthened me.
   b. The Word of the Lord came to prophets through visions and dreams.
   c. He asked if I was waiting for the undertaker or looking for the upper-taker.
   d. What the church needs on the mission field is exactly what the church needs at home.
   e. The disciples were transformed as a result of being eyewitnesses to the resurrection of Jesus Christ.

Exercises to Eliminate Harshness or Stridency

1. The purpose of this exercise is to learn how it feels to speak with a relaxed, open throat. Sip a deep breath as if through a straw, feeling how your throat opens with the inhalation. Now sigh a gentle, prolonged "ah," trying to keep the same open feeling in your throat that you felt on inhaling.

2. In contrast to the person who speaks with a breathy quality, harshness can often be the result of allowing too little air to escape on cer-

tain sounds. A good exercise, then, is one that combines a sound that requires an open throat with a sound that is being phonated harshly. Say the following words starting with "h," which requires the open throat. Listen particularly to the vowel sounds that follow the "h," making sure that the throat does not close back up and restrict the airflow during the production of the subsequent vowel sound.

hello	Haggai	how
heaven	happy	who
hope	horse	head

3. Read the following sentences, noting the relaxed position of the throat as you pronounce the "h" sound and then maintaining that same lack of tension through the rest of the sentence.

   a. Ho, every one who is thirsty.
   b. Hope is the anchor of the soul.
   c. Hello, and how are you this fine day?
   d. Happy are the people whose God is the Lord.
   e. How long shall I cry out for judgment?

4. Review the exercises to reduce tension included in the previous chapter. Harshness results from improper tension in the neck and throat, so learning to relax and release that tension should aid in the elimination of stridency. Practice the following relaxation exercises as well.

   a. Sit comfortably. Then consciously tighten all your muscles, drawing yourself together as if a whirlpool in the pit of your stomach were sucking everything into a black hole. Reverse the process and consciously release all tension, starting from the stomach and working out to the ends of all extremities.
   b. Extend the right arm stiffly into the air and let it fall loosely. Do the same with the left arm.
   c. Roll your head from the neck, first to the right several times and then to the left. Try to touch the shoulders, chest, and back as you rotate. At the same time, relax the jaw and let the mouth fall open.
   d. Slowly vocalize each of the vowel sounds, consciously eliminating any tension of the throat.
   e. Yawn and, keeping that same position, sing "Oh" at a comfortable pitch. Work to keep the tone constant, supported, and free from both breathiness and harshness. When the tone remains pure, you will have the right amount of tension in the throat.

5. Read the following selection, working constantly to maintain an open throat and eliminate any unnecessary tension. Keep the vowel sounds round. Elongate the vowel sounds if necessary to be certain the throat is open during phonation.

> O give thanks unto the LORD; for he is good: for his mercy endureth for ever. O give thanks unto the God of gods: for his mercy endureth for ever. O give thanks to the Lord of lords: for his mercy endureth for ever. To him who alone doeth great wonders: for his mercy endureth for ever. To him that by wisdom made the heavens: for his mercy endureth for ever. To him that stretched out the earth above the waters: for his mercy endureth for ever. To him that made great lights: for his mercy endureth for ever: The sun to rule by day: for his mercy endureth for ever. The moon and stars to rule by night: for his mercy endureth for ever *(Ps. 136:1-9)*.

6. Place a finger on top of your Adam's apple. Read the following sentence several times, allowing the larynx to move up and down naturally. If your finger loses contact as the Adam's apple moves up in the throat, keep practicing until you are able to lower the larynx to its natural position.

> "She saw the sun shining brightly on the cross."

7. Read each of the sentences below three times. The first time, tense the muscles of the throat and deliberately produce a harsh tone (don't overdo it; a sore throat is not the goal). The second time, eliminate all tension and deliberately allow extra air to escape, producing a breathy tone. The third time you read the sentence, try to achieve a balance, producing a full, rich, smooth tone.

   a. Never let it be said that you did less than your best for God.
   b. Glory surrounded the throne as the cherubim worshiped the King.
   c. The church that prays together, stays together.
   d. Christ taught us how to lead by showing us how to serve.
   e. Have you met with God in the garden of prayer?
   f. We don't just need to get deeper into the Bible, we need to get the Bible deeper into us.

Exercises for Elimination of Hoarseness

1. The first determination in dealing with hoarseness must be the identification of its cause. Hoarseness or chronic laryngitis may be

caused by influenza; allergies; nasal infections; smoking; or breathing second-hand smoke, dust, or other irritants in the air. If any of these are the cause of hoarseness, efforts must be made to deal with these medical or environmental factors.

2. A common cause of hoarseness for preachers lies in the abuse of the vocal folds, stemming from prolonged use of the speaking mechanism under conditions of nervous tension that affect the entire body. The solution for this can be found in the exercises for relaxation given in the previous chapter.

3. A third cause of chronic laryngitis involves improper tension localized in the speaking mechanism. Often this will surface toward the end of a sermon as the muscles of the voice grow tired from continued use. If that is the cause of your hoarseness, the following exercises should help overcome that problem.

4. To reduce tension in the larynx when speaking, stretch your head forward and downward, tensing your neck and jaw muscles. Let your head drop forward so that the chin touches the chest. Don't raise your shoulders as you move your head slowly to the right shoulder, to the rear, to the left, and forward again. As you rotate your head, gradually relax the jaw and neck muscles. Open the mouth and say "Lo, He comes," as you continue to rotate the head.

5. Repeat "ours" several times, opening the mouth widely as you speak.

6. Yawn with your mouth closed. (This is an exercise you can actually do on the platform while waiting to begin preaching.)

7. Determine your optimum pitch, the general pitch at which you speak most comfortably. "Imitation of others, a poor sense of pitch, various adverse personality characteristics, emotional disturbances, strain and nervous tension are among the factors that may contribute to the use of a faulty pitch level," according to Anderson.[13] People who speak habitually above or below their optimum pitch will find hoarseness resulting.

   a. To determine optimum pitch, sing an open "Ah" down the scale to the lowest note that can comfortably be vocalized. Then sing back up the scale five full steps. This should be your optimum pitch.

   b. Optimum pitch can also be discovered by relaxing the throat and singing an extended and relaxed "Ahhhh." Unless you are deliberately trying to match another tone, your voice should automatically sing at its optimum pitch.

c. A third way to help determine optimum pitch is to hold your hands over your ears and hum up and down the scale several times. One tone should stand out as being hummed with a rich, full tone. Compare that tone with the one you identified in the earlier exercises. They should be very close to the same pitch.

d. Experiment with this pitch by singing all of the vowel sounds. Try the pitches above and below to see if you feel more comfortable there.

e. Read the following sentence in a monotone, trying to make every sound in the sentence at the pitch you have identified as your optimum pitch. "This is the pitch level at which I speak most comfortably."

f. Read the sentence once again, allowing for inflection and expression. Notice whether your chosen optimum pitch allows for a range of pitch changes above and below the basic level while still allowing for comfort in the voice.

8. Use the following exercises to make your optimum pitch level habitual.

a. Chant the following sentences with a monotone, one-pitch voice, at your optimum pitch level. Concentrate on maintaining that single pitch level, however irritating it may sound.

(1) Every Sunday should start a new week.
(2) The world is full of opportunities disguised as problems.
(3) Young people are not the future church; they are the church.
(4) "My ways are not your ways, saith the LORD."
(5) The steps of a good man are also ordered by the Lord.

b. Read each sentence again. This time use natural expression, but be sure that the upward and downward inflections are centered around the optimum pitch you have identified. Do not allow the habitual vocal pitch to return to a higher or lower pitch level than what is most comfortable for you.

c. Without checking first, read a portion of Scripture at what you think is your optimum pitch. Record it if necessary. Avoid monotone; use natural expression. Then check the selection with your optimum pitch to see how close you were to what you identified

as most comfortable. Then go back to listen to one of the sermons you recorded and make the same comparison.

9. Hoarseness can be the result of trying to achieve loudness through
tension in the throat rather than support from the diaphragm muscles. Projection of tone should originate in the central region of the
body, not from the upper chest and neck. Use the following exercises
to determine the source of your loudness, and evaluate the effect of
that effort on your voice.

a. Shout the words, "GO! FIGHT! WIN!" three times. The first time,
imagine you are sitting at the edge of the basketball court and the
team is on the floor in front of you. The second time, you are at a
soccer game and the team is in the middle of the field. The third
time, you must be heard by the football team that is at the far end
of the field. Allow your pitch to seek its own level, and let the
sound explode. Especially on the third shout you will begin to
feel your voice rise in pitch and become strident in quality. Your
throat will probably be slightly irritated as well. You have just
demonstrated the two favorite, but improper, methods of achiev-
ing loudness: higher pitch and throat tension.

b. Speak sustained vowel sounds, gradually increasing and decreasing your volume while at the same time maintaining a constant
pitch level. Think of the support coming from the pressure produced by the diaphragm rather than any pressure in the throat.

c. Go to the auditorium where you normally preach. Imagine one
person sitting in the front row (I know it's hard to do that because no one ever sits there). Then imagine a person sitting in
the back row. Speak each of the following sentences twice. The
first time, speak so the person in the front row can hear you
clearly. The second time, support the tone so the person in the
back row can hear clearly. Avoid raising the pitch or tensing the
muscles in the throat.

(1) Rejoice in the day which the Lord has made.

(2) Does anyone have any prayer requests?

(3) The announcements today are all in the bulletin, so read them.

(4) Please open your Bibles to the 19th psalm.

(5) At this time the ushers will come forward to receive the offering.

10. Take a physical survey of your auditorium. Is it necessary for you to compete with other noises while preaching? Where is the nursery located? Is the heating or air conditioning system providing competition? Do you often preach with the windows open and compete with street noise? Do the floors squeak or amplify foot noise? Does the organ hum while not in use? Is the amplification system working properly? Do most of your people sit toward the back of the auditorium? All of these competing circumstances can contribute to hoarseness. Take steps to correct any of them that can possibly be corrected for the good of your voice.

Exercises for Elimination of Nasality and Denasality

1. Repeat the sounds "m" as in "mine," "n" as in "nine," and "ng" as in "sing." Sustain each sound as a hum, placing a finger on the ridge of the nose to feel the vibration of the nasal cavities and bones. These are the only three sounds that should cause such vibrations in the nose.

2. Vocalize the "n" sound, and then move into a combination with vowels. "Nah, nay, no, nigh, knee, new." Deliberately continue the nasal sound of the "n" as you vocalize the vowel. Then repeat the exercise, consciously changing from nasal to oral resonance as you move from the "n" to the vowel sound.

3. Concentrate on changing from oral to nasal sound as you vocalize the following sounds: "Own," "aim," "I'm," "iron," "earn," "him," "hymn," "sing," "ring."

4. Practice these words that move from nasal to oral resonance and then back to nasal: "Maim," "main," "men," "man," "mine," "ming," "moan."

5. Read aloud the following words, concentrating on a sense of vibration to alert you to the places where nasal resonance should normally be found. If necessary, place a finger on the bridge of the nose. "Solomon," "salvation," "singing," "sinning," "morning," "evening," "mingling," "mourning," "psalm," "psalms," "benediction."

6. "The following quotations from the Bible are so arranged that a line completely free of nasal consonants is followed by a line containing nasal consonants. See if you can differentiate between, and read the lines without nasal consonants so that nasal sounds are greatly minimized, if not completely eliminated: [Exercise from Stevenson and Diehl]

For the ear trieth words, as the palate tasteth food.
Therefore, hearken unto me, ye men of understanding.
Let us choose for us that which is right.
Man that is in honor and understandeth not,
Is like the beast that perisheth.
It was morning and it was evening one day.
Ye daughters of Israel, weep over Saul.
How are the mighty fallen in the midst of the battle.
Wherefore should I fear at the days of evil,
When iniquity at my heels compasseth me about?
They that trust to their wealth
And boast themselves in the multitude of their riches
This their way is their folly.
Yet after them men approve their saying.
Death shall be their shepherd,
And the upright shall have dominion over them in the morning."[14]

7. Watch yourself in a mirror as, with open mouth, you say first "Ah" and then "ng." Notice how the velum raises when you say "Ah." Notice how it lowers in order for you to say "ng." Get used to the feeling of this action so that you will recognize it when you encounter nasal consonants while preaching.

8. If you determined in your self-test that your problem lies in the area of denasality, or not including nasal resonance in the production of "m," "n," and "ng" sounds, work on the following exercises.

   a. Hum "m," "n," and "ng" up and down the scale. Notice the vibrations and become familiar with them.

   b. Read and reread the following words until you can definitely feel the vibrations in your nasal cavities and the bones of your nose as you speak.

same	sign	wane	wine
sin	moon	noon	ring
finger	heaven	mind	fling
grind	wind	poem	psalm
solemn	gloom	moan	strength

   c. Speak aloud the following sentences twice. The first time, exaggerate the nasal consonants, making the sounds vibrant and even elongating them. The second time, be aware of the nasal sounds, but speak them more normally.

(1) The king of Babylon worshiped the moon god.

(2) The moaning and the groaning of the tomb.

(3) Arrange for a marriage of common minds, blending man and maid.

(4) Then came storm and wind, completing God's command.

(5) The moon at noon promoted a solemn gloom.

Exercises for the Elimination of Throatiness or a Muffled Tone

1. Read the following psalm with your chin pulled down tight against your chest. Then read with the chin thrust awkwardly forward. Each time listen to the effect of such actions on your vocal tone.

    Make haste, O God, to deliver me; make haste to help me, O LORD. Let them be ashamed and confounded that seek after my soul; let them be turned backward, and put to confusion that desire my hurt. Let them be turned back for a reward of their shame that say, Aha, aha. Let all those that seek thee rejoice and be glad in thee: and let such as love thy salvation say continually, Let God be magnified. But I am poor and needy: make haste unto me, O God: thou art my help and my deliverer; O LORD, make no tarrying (Ps. 70:1-5).

2. Go back and review your sermon on video to see if you are subconsciously pulling your chin in toward your chest as you preach. If so, practice reading Scripture aloud in front of a mirror, forcing yourself to keep your head up and your chin away from the chest.

3. Check to see if your tongue position is correct; a faulty positioning of the tongue is often the cause of throatiness. Do the following exercises.

    a. Pull the tongue as far as possible back into the throat and read the following sentence: "Behold, the lamb of God, the promised Messiah of Israel."

    b. Read the sentence again, this time moving the tongue slightly forward. Fewer of the sounds should be garbled.

    c. Read the sentence a third time, pushing the tongue far forward in the mouth. Now you may have a problem with ability to articulate correctly as the tongue interferes with the position of the teeth and lips, but you will consciously be eliminating throatiness and a muffled tone.

4. Repeat each vowel five times. As you begin each repetition, pull the tongue to the back of the throat. Then move it slightly forward each time you repeat the vowel until the tongue is extending beyond the teeth. Become aware of the best position for the liveliest and brightest vowel sound.

   "a" as in "bay"
   "a" as in "saw"
   "e" as in "end"
   "e" as in "we"
   "i" as in "win"
   "i" as in "vine"
   "o" as in "open"
   "o" as in "cool"
   "o" as in "owl"
   "u" as in "up"

5. Throatiness or a muffled tone can also be the result of trying to speak at too low a pitch. Go back and review the exercises concerning optimum pitch in the previous section.

Exercises for the Elimination of Vocal Fry

1. Speak the following words with a downward sliding inflection. Start at a fairly high pitch, but slide quickly downward until you have reached the lowest possible pitch level. Then elongate the sound. If the voice starts to crack, you have identified the source of your vocal fry. Try the downward slide again, but this time stop at a pitch level just slightly higher than the place where the crackle in your voice began.

I'm	yes	when
boy	man	ours
day	ten	one
car	hand	new

2. Do just the opposite of what you did in exercise No. 1. Start the words with a gravelly rumble in the throat and slide the inflection upward. Raise the pitch slowly, and as soon as the vocal fry disappears from the word, hold the sound at that pitch for several seconds. Notice the improvement of the vocal quality at that particular pitch level.

awe	oh	law
mine	who	hymn
cause	worth	holy
sought	add	ask

FLEXIBILITY AND EXPRESSIVENESS

We have consistently emphasized that intensity of ideas is the best possible form of intensity. At the same time, those ideas may be ignored or misunderstood if not communicated with an intense delivery. The greatest incentive for a preacher to study the principles of oral communication lies in the increased effectiveness they offer in getting across his or her message. Simply developing a more flexible voice is not the goal. When people hear us preach, they should not marvel at the expressiveness of our voices; they should marvel at the grace that God conveys through our message.

Today's preacher faces competition for the attention of his or her audience from a great variety of sources. Not only do our people listen to the electronic church services on both radio and television, but they also hear some of the most able communicators in the world each evening on the news. Though there may not be any conscious comparisons between the local preacher and the media preacher, the standard for effectiveness is certainly higher than when the Sunday sermon was a community's only oral public communication during a week. Jerry Vines says that "as a result, the preacher has a harder time gaining and holding the attention of his people."[15]

Conveying emphasis is one reason for developing greater flexibility in the voice while preaching. Oral words cannot be underlined, capitalized, italicized, or placed in a bold font. All emphasis needs to come from paralanguage. A voice that lacks expressiveness will also lack emphasis. "Surely it must be a mortal sin to preach the gospel in a lackluster fashion,"[16] writes J. Daniel Baumann. Shouting and pounding the pulpit are not the only tools a preacher has to show emphasis in his or her sermon. In truth, they are probably the weakest weapons in the preacher's arsenal. A flexible, expressive voice will turn words into smart missiles that hone in on the listener and penetrate deeply into the mind and heart.

Gone are the days when a preacher sought to develop an oratorical tonal quality. The standard today and the goal for the modern pulpit could better be described as heightened conversation. We need to strive for what has often been called a storytelling quality. People want to feel as if the preacher is speaking directly to them. Intensity and passion are certainly appropriate, but only when they are centered in the intensity and passion of the subject matter.

Any sense on the part of an audience that the preacher is acting a role or inculcating false emotion into his or her sermon will quickly be perceived as hypocrisy. Preaching is not acting. A storyteller must be personal and connected with an audience. No dramatic "third wall" can be allowed to come between them. Pulpit communication must first of all be sincere. Advice from many years of teachers could be summarized this way: preaching from the mind will affect the mind of the listener; and preaching from the heart will affect the heart of the listener; but preaching from the life will affect the life of the listener.

It would be nice if sincerity were the sum total of all that a preacher needed to consider, but it is not. Even the most sincere individuals do not always sound sincere. The most passionate people do not always have voices that convince others of their passion. People whose minds abound with energetic ideas often possess voices that lull you to sleep with repetitive monotony. "If you bore the jury, you have lost the case,"[17] asserts David Larsen.

In spite of living all your life with the voice you were born with, you probably don't have a real good idea how you sound. The process of actually recording your voice and listening to yourself may have provided a real shock to your system. Most students go into immediate denial when they first hear their voices on tape, making comments such as, "That's not really what I sound like, is it?" With the high fidelity of modern recording equipment, just mark it down. That is what you sound like.

Conversational quality will result in an expressive voice that is purposeful. Closely related to sincerity, purposefulness reminds us that "people should speak not because they have to but because they want to."[18] An audience must always sense in the preacher's voice a sense of purpose. They must know that this message is one that has first of all touched the preacher's heart before being shared with them. A dull, unexpressive voice will never be able to communicate such a purpose. That doesn't mean the heart has not been touched; it simply means that the inflexible voice is successfully hiding the heart from the congregation.

For the next series of self-tests, listen very carefully to the sound of your voice. Concentrate on what you are doing, but think also about what your voice is able to do. Every preacher can improve in the area of flexibility and expressiveness with practice just as Robert Cohen urges actors to improve: "Stage speaking is to daily conversation what Olympic high hurdling is to the morning jog; it demands training and conditioning as well as above-average gifts."[19] Even if a person were to determine that no major problems were present in the area of expressiveness, it would be prudent to plan out a series of exercises to keep the voice flexible and in top-notch condition.

While taking the following self-tests, try to listen to several sermons, paying particular attention to the vocal patterns involved in volume, pacing, pitch, and quality. To help you concentrate on the specific sound patterns, you may want to alternate between the use of the audio and video recordings. Turn them up almost to an uncomfortable level so that you cannot ignore any of the incidental sounds being produced by your voice. Try to listen critically, from outside yourself. Always compare the paralanguage with the language, asking yourself, "Does the expressiveness of my voice reinforce or detract from the emotional content of my message? Is my voice hiding or revealing what is really in my heart?"

Self-Test for Analyzing Expressiveness

Rate: Pacing and Pause

1. Choose a portion of one sermon that you think is spoken at an average rate of speed. Count the number of words spoken in one minute, using the written transcript of the message as well as the audio recording. Do this at several different points throughout the sermon and average the results. What is your average rate of words per minute (w.p.m.)? _____

2. Choose one minute from the beginning, one minute from the middle, and one minute from the end of your sermon, and count the words spoken during each of those minutes, using the written transcript.
   Beginning _____
   Middle   _____
   Ending   _____

3. Using the same method, determine the average words per minute of your normal conversation. _____

4. Listen closely to your sermon to see if any regular speech patterns are apparent. Answer the following questions as you listen.

a. What type of rhythm is suggested by the pattern of your words: march, waltz, rapid-fire, irregular? _____

b. Do you sustain some vowel sounds longer than others? If so, which? _____

c. Do you sustain some words longer than others? If so, which?

_____

d. Which word in each pair best describes your rate of speaking?

regular   irregular
patterned   varied
boring   interesting

5. Listen to one sermon, and react to the following statements.

a. When the mood of the sermon changes, does my rate change?
    Yes   No

b. Do my words ever flow so rapidly that I run sounds together?
    Yes   No

c. Do I find my mind wandering to other matters when I listen to myself preach?
    Yes   No

d. Do I come to full stops at the end of every sentence?
    Yes   No

e. Do parts of the sermon sound like one run-on sentence?
    Yes   No

f. Do I expand or elongate words that evoke a sense of reverence?
    Yes   No

g. Do I speak quickly those words that evoke a sense of joy?
    Yes   No

h. Do I expand or elongate words that evoke a sense of rage?
    Yes   No

i. Do I speak quickly words that evoke a sense of grief?
    Yes   No

j. Do I elongate or expand words that evoke a sense of calmness?
    Yes   No

k. Do I speak quickly words that evoke a sense of enthusiasm?
    Yes   No

l. Do I hear myself pausing in the middle of phrases where the idea really continues on to the next words?
    Yes   No

m. Do all of my words run together without the insertion of any pauses?
    Yes   No

   n. Do my pauses always occur in places where I need to breathe?

       Yes   No

   o. Do I ever substitute a look and a pause in place of words?

       Yes   No

   p. Does my overall rate of speaking interfere with the clarity of words?

       Yes   No

   q. Does my overall rate of speaking evoke a sense of sameness?

       Yes   No

   r. Do I ever pause after a phrase to underscore what has just been said?

       Yes   No

   s. Do I ever pause before an idea to heighten suspense?

       Yes   No

   t. Does my rate of speaking correspond with the emotional content of the message?

       Yes   No

   u. Does my rate of speaking interfere with the intelligibility of the message?

       Yes   No

   v. Does my rate of speaking keep the attention of the listener?

       Yes   No

   w. Does my rate of speaking make me want to tell myself to hurry up?

       Yes   No

   x. Have I used a variety of rates of speaking throughout the sermon?

       Yes   No

SCORING:

1. If your average words per minute fall within the 140 to 180 w.p.m. range, you are speaking at an average rate of speed. If your average is lower or higher than that, use the following exercises to help yourself become comfortable with the standard, conversational rate of public speaking. Exceptions to that rate of speaking would occur when the subject material calls for a slower or faster rate due to its emotional content. If your sermon subject dealt with joy and excitement, you might naturally expect to have a rate above 180 w.p.m. If it dealt with grief or highly technical language, you might fall below 140. If you be-

lieve the subject matter to be a deciding factor, perform the experiment again with a different sermon to determine your basic rate of speaking.

2. The introduction, conclusion, and body of the message would normally vary in their mood and emotional content. If you found that your rate of speaking was constant or nearly the same at all three points in the message, it may suggest that you are not using a great deal of variety in your pacing. Choose exercises that will help you match your rate of speech to the emotional mood of the message you are seeking to enhance through paralanguage.

3. Comparing your rate of speaking in normal conversation to that of your public communication will show you whether or not platform tension is causing you to rush your words. A person may of course speak too rapidly or too slowly in normal conversation as well. Use the comparison as a guide to the overall pace of your preaching. Evaluate that pace in regard to how well you believe it helps you maintain the attention of your listeners. Remember that most people think at somewhere near 800 w.p.m. So even if you are speaking at 180 w.p.m., they can think about 620 words faster. That doesn't mean they can pay attention to all those words, but they can hear them.

4. Look at your answers and ask yourself if they suggest the presence of a speech pattern related to pacing in your delivery. If so, make use of the exercises that help develop vocal variety in this area. Sameness bores.

5. When scoring the fifth part of the self-test, give yourself 1 point for each answer listed below. More than 20 points suggests that you are using fairly good vocal variety in your pacing. A score of 20 points or less should encourage you to give attention to the exercises for the improvement of pacing.
   a. Yes
   b. No
   c. No
   d. No
   e. No
   f. Yes
   g. Yes
   h. No
   i. No

j. Yes

k. Yes

l. No

m. No

n. No

o. Yes

p. No

q. No

r. Yes

s. Yes

t. Yes

u. No

v. Yes

w. No

x. Yes

Exercises for the Improvement of Pacing

1. A speaking rate below 140 w.p.m. may be appropriate for eulogies and complex scientific lectures, but it will irritate the average Sunday morning audience. They will think the speaker is either ill or thinking very slowly. To get the feel of a very slow rate of speaking, read the following 92-word selection. Keep one eye on a clock, and make yourself use a full minute in reading the material.

   And when I came to you, brethren, I did not come with superiority of speech or of wisdom, proclaiming to you the testimony of God. For I determined to know nothing among you except Jesus Christ, and Him crucified. And I was with you in weakness and in fear and in much trembling. And my message and my preaching were not in persuasive words of wisdom, but in demonstration of the Spirit and of power, that your faith should not rest on the wisdom of men, but on the power of God *(1 Cor. 2:1-5, NASB)*.

2. A speaking rate above 180 w.p.m. may tire your listeners, since they are not used to consuming oral material at such a rapid rate, even though they are mentally capable of doing so. Rapid pacing suggests that a person is unsure and nervous. In everyday terminology a "fast talker" is not someone people trust. A rapid rate as a means of variety has its place, but it should not characterize your basic pace as a preacher. To get the feel of a rapid rate of speech, read the following

selection that contains 230 words. Time yourself and complete the entire paragraph within one minute.

How lovely are Thy dwelling places, O Lord of hosts! My soul longed and even yearned for the courts of the Lord; my heart and my flesh sing for joy to the living God. The bird also has found a house, and the swallow a nest for herself, where she may lay her young, even Thine altars, O Lord of hosts, my King and my God. How blessed are those who dwell in Thy house! They are ever praising Thee. How blessed is the man whose strength is in Thee; in whose heart are the highways to Zion! Passing through the valley of Baca, they make it a spring, the early rain also covers it with blessings. They go from strength to strength, every one of them appears before God in Zion. O Lord God of hosts, hear my prayer; give ear, O God of Jacob! Behold our shield, O God, and look upon the face of Thine anointed. For a day in Thy courts is better than a thousand outside. I would rather stand at the threshold of the house of my God, than dwell in the tents of wickedness. For the Lord God is a sun and shield; the Lord gives grace and glory; no good thing does He withhold from those who walk uprightly. O Lord of hosts, how blessed is the man who trusts in Thee! *(Ps. 84:1-12, NASB).*

3. General conversational delivery in public speaking should aim at a basic rate of approximately 160 w.p.m. That does not rule out variety in pace, but that basic rate will feel most comfortable to your listeners. To get a feel of that rate, read the following selection that contains 156 words. Time yourself and complete the entire paragraph within one minute.

And He began to teach again by the sea. And such a very great multitude gathered to Him that He got into a boat in the sea and sat down; and the whole multitude was by the sea on the land. And He was teaching them many things in parables, and was saying to them in His teaching, "Listen to this! Behold, the sower went out to sow; and it came about that as he was sowing, some seed fell beside the road, and the birds came and ate it up. And other seed fell on the rocky ground where it did not have much soil; and immediately it sprang up because it had no depth of soil. And after the sun had risen, it was scorched; and because it had no root, it withered away. And other seed fell among the thorns, and the thorns came up and choked it, and it yielded no crop" *(Mark 4:1-7, NASB).*

4. More important than your basic rate of speech is the use of vocal variety in pacing. Look closely at the following verses and decide on a general rate that best fits the mood of the material—rapid, slow, or regular. Then read each one aloud, maintaining that basic rate but also increasing and decreasing your pace for emphasis.

   a. "And there were following Him a great multitude of the people, and of women who were mourning and lamenting Him. But Jesus turning to them said, 'Daughters of Jerusalem, stop weeping for Me, but weep for yourselves and for your children'" (Luke 23:27-28, NASB).

   b. "Son of man, prophesy against the prophets of Israel who prophesy, and say to those who prophesy from their own inspiration, Listen to the word of the LORD!" (Ezek. 13:2, NASB).

   c. "Who is like Thee among the gods, O LORD? Who is like Thee, majestic in holiness, awesome in praises, working wonders?" (Exod. 15:11, NASB).

   d. "No temptation has overtaken you but such as is common to man; and God is faithful, who will not allow you to be tempted beyond what you are able; but with the temptation will provide the way of escape also, that you may be able to endure it" (1 Cor. 10:13, NASB).

   e. "Thus I hated all the fruit of my labor for which I had labored under the sun, for I must leave it to the man who will come after me. And who knows whether he will be a wise man or a fool? Yet he will have control over all the fruit of my labor for which I have labored by acting wisely under the sun. This too is vanity" (Eccles. 2:18-19, NASB).

5. In the following selections, pause at every place marked with a slash (/), but breathe only when you need to. After reading the sentences with the pauses, go back and reread them without pausing. There will be a great difference.

   a. If everyone who ever went to sleep in church were laid end to end, / they would be a lot more comfortable.

   b. That that is / is. / That that is not / is not. / But that that is not is not that that is, / neither is that that is / that that is not.

   c. There are 10 ways to turn a bad day into a good day. / No. 1: / find someone who needs your help and help him or her. / Then repeat that 10 times.

d. "For from Him / and through Him / and to Him / are all things. / To Him be the glory / forever. / Amen" (Rom. 11:36, NASB).

e. "Managers are people who do things right, / and leaders / are people who do the right thing."[20]

6. Using duration for emphasis can produce an irritating type of paralanguage called a speech pattern. Personal speech patterns can be very hard to identify because they are so familiar. Work through the following exercises, and ask yourself if speech patterns are a habitual part of your preaching. If they are, becoming aware of them will be the first step in eliminating them.

a. Read the following, pausing and breathing at each slash (/) mark.
   (1) A B C / D E F / G H I / J K L / M N O / P Q R
   (2) A B C D / E F G H / I J K L / M N O P / Q R S T
   (3) A B C D E F G / H I J K L M N / O P Q R S T U

b. Read the following sentence and deliberately lengthen or elongate the sound of the word "Lord" every time it appears.

   O Lord, You are my Lord, and I will ever seek You. I will
   search for You in the morning, Lord. O Lord, be not far from me.

c. Go back to the list of words in self-test No. 4 that you identified as words you tend to elongate regularly. Say each word aloud 10 times, trying to give the word a different duration each time.

7. The best solution to problems with rate lies in a proper understanding of your message and a desire to communicate that understanding to an audience. Pacing must fit the mood of the matters being discussed, and pauses must occur in places that emphasize and call attention to what is being said. Read through the following selection, and mark the places appropriate for pauses. Underline words that you intend to emphasize by giving them added time. Then read it aloud using an appropriate rate of speed, duration of words for emphasis, and proper phrasing for understanding.

   Then David said to himself, "Now I will perish one day by the hand of Saul. There is nothing better for me than to escape into the land of the Philistines. Saul then will despair of searching for me anymore in all the territory of Israel, and I will escape from his hand." So David arose and crossed over, he and the six hundred men who were with him, to Achish the son of Maoch, king of

Gath. And David lived with Achish at Gath, he and his men, each with his household, even David with his two wives, Ahinoam the Jezreelitess, and Abigail the Carmelitess, Nabal's widow. Now it was told Saul that David fled to Gath, so he no longer searched for him. Then David said to Achish, "If now I have found favor in your sight, let them give me a place in one of the cities in the country, that I may live there; for why should your servant live in the royal city with you?" So Achish gave him Ziklag that day; therefore Ziklag has belonged to the kings of Judah to this day. And the number of the days that David lived in the country of the Philistines was a year and four months *(1 Sam. 27:1-7, NASB)*.

Self-Test for Analyzing Expressiveness

Volume

1. Place a television and video player on the platform of the auditorium where you normally preach. Turn the volume up to what you consider to be a normal level. While watching the sermon, move to a different part of the auditorium every five minutes. This will not be a perfect test because people who listen to you on Sunday morning cannot adjust the volume. But use it to answer the following questions.

    a. Is there any place in the auditorium where my voice is hard to hear?

       Yes   No

    b. Is there any place in the auditorium where I feel overwhelmed by the volume of my voice?

       Yes   No

    c. Do I ever have to strain to hear the end of individual sentences?

       Yes   No

    d. Does my volume overall seem too soft for the room?

       Yes   No

    e. Does my volume overall seem too loud for the room?

       Yes   No

    f. Do I use any volume that could be described as a shout?

       Yes   No

    g. Does that shouting occur more often than once every five minutes or so?

       Yes   No

h. Do I use any volume that could be described as a whisper?

     Yes   No

i. Does my whispering occur more often than every five minutes or so?

     Yes   No

j. Did you ever want to adjust the volume on the VCR up while listening?

     Yes   No

k. Did you ever want to adjust the volume down on the VCR while listening?

     Yes   No

l. Is an increase in volume your favorite method of emphasizing words?

     Yes   No

m. Do I use volume for emphasis of individual words more often than once a minute?

     Yes   No

2. Identify a portion of a sermon where you felt it necessary to increase the volume of your voice. Listen to that portion several times and respond to the following questions.

a. Do my facial expressions and increased volume make me appear to be angry?

     Yes   No

b. Do I detect any mechanical distortion in the amplification equipment as a result of my shouting?

     Yes   No

c. Does the pitch level of my voice rise every time the volume increases?

     Yes   No

d. Does the combination of facial expression and volume suggest a person who sounds disgusted with those who listen?

     Yes   No

e. In retrospect, was volume the best way to add emphasis at this particular point in the sermon?

     Yes   No

f. Although appropriate, was volume the only way to emphasize the material?

     Yes   No

g. Was my volume great enough to cause someone using a hearing aid any pain?

Yes   No

3. Identify a portion of the sermon where you consciously decreased volume for a period of time. Listen to that portion several times and respond to the following questions.

a. In retrospect, did you deliberately decrease your volume for the purpose of emphasizing the message?

Yes   No

b. Is the decrease in volume accompanied by a lack of intensity in the voice?

Yes   No

c. Does the decrease in volume interfere with intelligibility?

Yes   No

d. Is the decrease in volume accompanied by a lack of precision in articulation?

Yes   No

e. Does the subject matter that is whispered seem so important that people will pay closer attention in order to hear what is being said?

Yes   No

f. Does it sound as if you are speaking more softly just because you lack proper breath support?

Yes   No

4. Listen to your sermon, paying particular attention to the stress or emphasis given to individual words. Respond to the following statements as you listen.

a. Do I emphasize so many words that none of them stand out?

Yes   No

b. Is volume the only method I use for emphasis?

Yes   No

c. Do I emphasize some words every time they occur, regardless of whether or not they deserve emphasis at that particular place?

Yes   No

d. Do I seem to emphasize words randomly, without a definite reason?

Yes   No

e. Do I emphasize words deliberately, thus increasing audience understanding?

Yes   No

f. Are most of the words I emphasize nouns and verbs?

  Yes No

g. Are most of the words I emphasize pronouns, prepositions, and conjunctions?'

  Yes No

SCORING:

1. For No. 1, if you answered *yes* to *a, b, c, d, e, j,* or *k,* you need to look at the exercises concerning projection of the voice. If you answered *no* to *f, h,* or *m,* and *yes* to *g, i,* or *l,* you need to look at the exercises concerning the use of volume for expressiveness.

2. For No. 2, if you answered *yes* to *a, b, c, d,* or *g;* or *no* to *e* or *f,* choose exercises that will help you overcome the excessive use of volume as a means of emphasis and use it instead as a means of expressiveness.

3. For No. 3, if you answered *yes* to *a, b, c, d,* or *f;* and *no* to *e,* choose exercises that will help you increase your use of volume as a means of emphasis as well as a means of expressiveness.

4. For No. 4, give yourself 1 point for each *no* answer to *a, b, c, d,* or *g,* and 1 point for each *yes* answer to *e* and *f.* If your total is less than a perfect 7, work on the exercises that will help you use volume effectively as a means of emphasis in your preaching.

Exercises for Improvement in Volume

1. "Genuine spiritual power in the pulpit is not synonymous with loudness. Hard hearts are not likely to be broken by shrill voices,"[21] concludes John Piper. If your self-analysis suggests that you are overusing volume as a means of emphasis, go back and practice the exercises for relaxation in chapter 5. A tense body will produce a tense voice.

2. Constant use of volume will also result in abuse of the vocal folds. Review the exercises for stridency and hoarseness earlier in this chapter. Such vocal problems almost always accompany excessive volume in preaching.

3. Stress is the amount of emphasis given to a syllable within a word. The use of stress is an appropriate means of using volume for emphasis. Just remember that when you stress every syllable, nothing is em-

phasized. Stress should be used to increase intelligibility, not just to force a listener to pay attention because of increased volume. Read the following words, giving stress to the underlined syllables by the use of increased volume. Notice how stress can actually change the meaning of the word.

rebel	creator	Megiddo
rebel	Calvary	savior
convict	crucifixion	salvation
convict	Golgotha	regeneration
project	Habakkuk	pharaoh
project	Mississippi	originate

4. Read aloud the following sentences. Notice the difference in meaning that results from stressing different words.
   a. The Cross is the way to God.
   b. The Cross is the way to God.
   c. The Cross is the way to God.
   d. The Cross is the way to God.
   e. The Cross is the way to God.

5. Read each of the following statements twice. The first time, use volume to emphasize the underlined phrase. The second time, emphasize the other part of the statement. Notice the sometimes subtle differences that result.
   a. Felix said, "Sometime I will listen to you. But not today."
   b. God will give me strength when I trust in Him.
   c. Isaiah prophesied the captivity of Israel. He knew it would happen.
   d. When Christ died on the Cross, Satan celebrated, and the disciples mourned.
   e. "The first to plead a cause seems just, until another comes and examines him" (Prov. 18:17, NASB).
   f. "Better is a dry morsel and quietness with it than a house full of feasting with strife" (Prov. 17:1, NASB).
   g. "A fool always loses his temper, but a wise man holds it back" (Prov. 29:11, NASB).

6. Read the following sentences twice. The first time, stress the indicated word; the second time, choose a different word for emphasis.
   a. God expects us to live by faith.

   b. No matter <u>where</u> you are going, once you get there, there you are.

   c. He said he would go to church with <u>her.</u>

   d. How <u>many</u> times do I have to tell you?

   e. If God <u>had</u> to choose one service to attend, it would be prayer meeting.

   f. Some people never put off till tomorrow what they can put off till the <u>next</u> day.

   g. God is not nearly as concerned about who will help Him, as He is about who will accept <u>His</u> help.

Self-Test for Analyzing Expressiveness

Pitch

1. Using a piano or other instrument, try to match the pitch levels of your voice. Do this at different places within a sermon, 8 or 10 at a time. If you don't play an instrument, get someone to help you. Write the pitch levels by their letter names, or place them on a musical scale. Then answer the following questions.

   a. What pitch occurs most often? _____

   b. What is the highest note in your speaking range? _____

   c. What is the lowest note in your speaking range? _____

   d. How many different pitch levels do you use? _____

   e. Do you ever change pitch levels within words? _____

   f. Do you ever change pitch levels between words? _____

   g. In musical terms, would you be a bass, baritone, second tenor, or first tenor? _____

   h. Is there a repetitious pattern in your pitch levels? _____

2. Listen to an entire sermon, either on cassette, video, or CD, paying particular attention to the sound of your voice. As you listen, consider the following statements.

   a. Does my pitch drop off at the end of sentences?

         Yes   No

   b. Does my voice crack or break when the pitch drops at the end of sentences?

         Yes   No

   c. Does every sentence end on about the same pitch without dropping?

         Yes   No

  d. Even if I do drop the pitch at the end of sentences, does the end of each sentence sound the same?

    Yes No

  e. Does my speaking voice sound significantly lower than my normal voice?

    Yes No

  f. Does my speaking voice sound significantly higher than my normal voice?

    Yes No

  g. When I raise my pitch for strong emphasis, is the emphasized pitch only slightly higher than my optimum or normal pitch?

    Yes No

  h. Does my voice have a thin or weak quality when I preach?

    Yes No

  i. Does my voice have a harsh or strident quality when I preach?

    Yes No

  j. Does my voice have a nasal quality when I preach?

    Yes No

  k. Do I start every sentence at a higher pitch and then drop the pitch lower as I continue on with the sentence?

    Yes No

  l. Do I ever end sentences on a rising pitch when they are not questions?

    Yes No

  m. Do I hear any repeated patterns of inflection within sentences?

    Yes No

3. Take a large sheet of paper. Draw a straight line across the entire sheet to represent your optimum pitch. Starting at the left end of the line, chart the sound of your voice while listening to one of your recorded sermons. Allow your pencil to flow freely, matching the upward and downward inflection of the voice, above and below the centerline. Do this for a period of five minutes or more, using additional paper if necessary. Include punctuation so that you can later identify the beginning and end of sentences and phrases. Then look back over the graph you have prepared and respond to the following statements.

  a. Do I spend most of my time above my optimum pitch?

    Yes No

    b. Do I spend most of my time below my optimum pitch?
        Yes   No
    c. Do I use a narrow range of pitches while preaching?
        Yes   No
    d. Do I use a wide range of pitches while preaching?
        Yes   No
    e. Do I see a pattern of inflection occurring at the end of sentences?
        Yes   No
    f. Do I see a pattern of inflection occurring at the beginning of sentences?
        Yes   No
    g. Do I see large repetitions of pitch patterns emerging in the graph?
        Yes   No

4. Answer each of the following questions based upon your observations concerning the use of pitch while preaching.
    a. Is my overall pitch higher or lower than in normal conversation?
    b. How predictable is the pitch variation I use?
    c. Do I come anywhere near to using the potential range of my voice?
    d. Have I developed a "ministerial tone" that reveals itself in the patterns of pitch I use while preaching?
    e. Would the pitch variety I use while preaching sound strange if I used the same patterns during everyday conversation?
    f. Do I sound solemn and hushed no matter what subject I may be discussing?
    g. Do I frequently raise the pitch of my voice at the end of sentences in order to maintain a sense of dignity and solemnity?
    h. Does the pitch variety in my voice adequately express the emotion contained in the words I am saying?
    i. Does my pitch variety call attention to itself because it is overdone?

SCORING:

1. The following comments will help you analyze and understand your responses to the first part of the self-test.
    a. The pitch that occurs most often is probably your optimum pitch.
    b. If this note is not seven or eight notes above your optimum pitch, you either have too high an optimum pitch or you are not using the upper part of your range effectively.

    c. If this note is not seven or eight notes below your optimum pitch, you either have too low an optimum pitch or you are not using the lower part of your range effectively.

    d. This will vary, but the average voice is capable of a speaking range of about two octaves.

    e. Pitch levels within words are called slurs, and they are very necessary for proper inflection.

    f. Pitch levels between words are called steps, and they are likewise necessary for proper inflection.

    g. This will vary, but your singing voice should be in the same range as the optimum pitch of your speaking voice.

    h. Pitch patterns are the great foe of vocal expressiveness. Any patterns you develop will lead to monotony in expression that will in turn cause you to lose the attention of an audience.

2 and 3. Give yourself 1 point for each of the indicated answers. Any more than 3 total points will indicate that you would do well to pay attention to the following exercises for the improvement of pitch variety.

Test No. 2	*Test No. 3*
a. No	a. Yes
b. Yes	b. Yes
c. Yes	c. Yes
d. Yes	d. No
e. Yes	e. Yes
f. Yes	f. Yes
g. Yes	g. Yes
h. Yes	
i. Yes	
j. Yes	
k. Yes	
l. Yes	
m. Yes	

4. For test No. 4, your answers to these questions will obviously vary. However, if you are personally convinced that you could profit from greater pitch flexibility in your voice, choose from the following exercises and plan your own program for improvement.

Exercises for Improvement in Pitch Variety

1. Sitting at a piano, find a note that is easy for you to hum. Then play down the scale and hum the notes to the lowest comfortable pitch. Starting there, play notes and hum up the scale to the highest comfortable pitch. You should have a total range of 12 to 16 notes or more.

2. Speak your way up the scale. Start the following sentence at a comfortably low pitch. Each word should then be spoken at the next pitch level until you have moved as high on the scale as is comfortable. You should be able to read each word at a pitch level higher than the previous word.

   "The message of Christ has gone out to the end of the world."

3. Repeat the same sentence, this time starting at the top of your range and speaking your way down the scale. Read each word at a pitch level lower than the previous word.

4. Practice the following sentences, moving up or down the scale from where you begin. Alternate exercises, starting one sentence at a low pitch and the next at a high pitch.

   a. You don't say.

   b. Never in a million years.

   c. Do we really want to see revival?

   d. Do good unto all men—God loves them all.

   e. It will be worth it all when we see Christ in His glory.

   f. The announcements printed in the bulletin will be read aloud anyway.

   g. The man of faith will greet each day with confidence, knowing and trusting the God who cannot fail.

5. Basic pitch level should change with our emotions. Excitement, humor, and good cheer are usually expressed by a higher pitch. Casual conversation is usually carried on at a medium pitch range. Grief, melancholy, love, and intense logic often call for the use of lower pitches. But even within these general pitch ranges, a person should use variety. Read the following scriptures silently. Mentally choose a pitch that will best express the overall emotion of the selection. Then read the verses aloud, using the chosen pitch to help express the mood of the subject.

a. Thus says the LORD, "Cursed is the man who trusts in mankind and makes flesh his strength, and whose heart turns away from the LORD. For he will be like a bush in the desert and will not see when prosperity comes, but will live in stony wastes in the wilderness, a land of salt without inhabitant. Blessed is the man who trusts in the LORD and whose trust is the LORD. For he will be like a tree planted by the water, that extends its roots by a stream and will not fear when the heat comes; but its leaves will be green, and it will not be anxious in a year of drought nor cease to yield fruit *(Jer. 17:5-8, NASB)*.

b. Then I was very angry when I had heard their outcry and these words. And I consulted with myself, and contended with the nobles and the rulers and said to them, "You are exacting usury, each from his brother!" Therefore, I held a great assembly against them. And I said to them, "We according to our ability have redeemed our Jewish brothers who were sold to the nations; now would you even sell your brothers that they may be sold to us?" Then they were silent and could not find a word to say. Again I said, "The thing which you are doing is not good; should you not walk in the fear of our God because of the reproach of the nations, our enemies?" *(Neh. 5:6-9, NASB)*.

c. Like an apple tree among the trees of the forest, so is my beloved among the young men. In his shade I took great delight and sat down, and his fruit was sweet to my taste. He has brought me to his banquet hall, and his banner over me is love. Sustain me with raisin cakes, refresh me with apples, because I am lovesick. Let his left hand be under my head and his right hand embrace me *(Song of Sol. 2:3-6, NASB)*.

d. So then, my beloved, just as you have always obeyed, not as in my presence only, but now much more in my absence, work out your salvation with fear and trembling; for it is God who is at work in you, both to will and to work for His good pleasure. Do all things without grumbling or disputing; that you may prove yourselves to be blameless and innocent children of God above reproach in the midst of a crooked and perverse generation, among whom you appear as lights in the world, holding fast the word of life, so that in the day of Christ I may have cause to glory because I did not run in vain nor toil in vain. But even if I am being poured out as a drink offering upon the sacrifice and service of your faith, I rejoice and share my joy with you all. And you too, I urge you, rejoice in the same way and share your joy with me *(Phil. 2:12-18, NASB)*.

6. "Inflection" is the word used to describe a change in pitch within a word. The inflection used within a word can completely change the meaning of that word. Read each of the following words, first with an upward inflection, then with a downward inflection, and finally with a circumflex, or both upward and downward, inflection. Exaggerate in order to become comfortable with pitch variety.

   a. one
   b. who
   c. heaven
   d. forever
   e. why
   f. peace
   g. love
   h. joy
   i. longsuffering
   j. good
   k. meek
   l. lion

7. Say the word *no,* but by using inflection make it suggest the following meanings.

   a. Great excitement
   b. Extreme fear
   c. Sarcasm
   d. Approval
   e. Curiosity
   f. Calculated indifference
   g. Amazement
   h. Embarrassment

8. When a speaker changes pitch between words, it is called a "step." A step can be a change of one tone or several tones in either direction. Practice saying each of the following statements twice. The first time, step up between the words, and the second time, step down.

   a. Don't go!
   b. I see.
   c. Never again.
   d. This time.
   e. The end.
   f. Try this.
   g. Now what.
   h. He didn't.

9. When one of the syllables within a word is spoken on a higher pitch, that is referred to as "stress." The volume of the sound is usually in-

creased slightly as well. The use of stress makes a speaker much more understandable because it increases the clarity of the spoken word. Read the following words, stressing the underlined syllable by raising the pitch of the voice.

a. <u>Ni</u>san
b. Me<u>mor</u>ial
c. Jo<u>si</u>ah
d. Con<u>vict</u>
e. Intertesta<u>men</u>tal
f. Pro<u>ject</u>
g. <u>Pro</u>ject
h. Halle<u>lu</u>jah

10. When an entire group of words are stressed, this is usually referred to as "emphasis." Pitch is one of the most effective ways of emphasizing a phrase. Usually when speakers use pitch for emphasis, they favor a rise in pitch, but don't neglect the use of a lower pitch combined with softer volume for emphasis. Often that will be just as effective as its opposite. Read each of the following sentences twice. The first time, emphasize the underlined phrase by a rise in pitch. Then try it again with a lower pitch for emphasis and see which is the most effective.

a. Never give up! <u>Never give up!</u>
b. I refuse. <u>Don't ask me again.</u>
c. "Rejoice in the Lord always: <u>and again I say, Rejoice"</u> (Phil. 4:4).
d. <u>I told you so.</u> I knew he would do it.
e. Experience is <u>not the best teacher.</u>
f. The Sunday morning sermon, <u>when it becomes necessary,</u> may be concluded the following week.

11. You have stopped while on vacation to visit an old friend and hear him preach. After the service you greet him at the door with the words, "What a sermon. I've never heard anything quite like that before." Use inflection to practice saying that sentence with the following meanings.

a. The sermon was truly outstanding.
b. The sermon was delivered well, but the subject matter bordered on heresy.
c. You are teasing him by suggesting the sermon was awful.
d. You were surprised by the improvement over the last time you heard him preach.
e. The sermon subject was one you have never heard from a pulpit.

7
Dedicating Yourself

■ The variables that impact preaching change not only from one preacher to another but also from week to week for each individual. A program of planned preaching will help cushion the effect these variables have on the pastor's time. But no program can completely eliminate the frustration of those weeks when interruptions leave little time for sermon preparation. Who hasn't encountered the unexpected funeral or an unusual demand for hospital visitation? Lowell Erdahl reminds us, "When you are well prepared, you preach; when you are not well prepared, you preach anyway."[1]

The greatest obstacle to improving your sermon delivery will be the tyranny of time, the same enemy you face in sermon preparation. Lack of time must never be an excuse if the real culprit is laziness, however. The time needed each week to exegete a passage and prepare an outline or write a narrative manuscript takes natural precedence over time spent in oral exercises. Yet both are necessary, and the effective communicator will neglect neither one. Just as you preach when your preparation time is curtailed, so you preach when time spent on your delivery is cut short. Though, that should not keep you from spending more time working on both the next week.

A preacher should not attempt to incorporate everything from this book into his or her preaching in just a few weeks. Immediate improvement in delivery will be noticeable as the exercises are used, but continued improvement is a lifetime task. A person who develops a musical skill must continually seek improvement or risk losing whatever was already mastered. Even so, improvement of delivery should be the unceasing focus of the preacher who desires effective communication skills.

Just as time factors differ from ministry to ministry, so do the personality traits of communicators. Case studies of those using the exercises in this book have revealed several obstacles that varied according to the personalities of the individuals using the self-tests. None of them were insurmountable. Just being aware of them should help a preacher more effectively analyze and improve his or her delivery.

THE OBSTACLE OF GENERAL LAZINESS

Several of the case studies were conducted in homiletics classes. This provided an opportunity to compare the use of the self-tests to the general preparation for classroom assignments. Not surprisingly, those students who dedicated more time to the preparation phase of homiletics were also more likely to engage in significant self-analysis using the self-tests. Those who submitted work on time and scored well in the exegesis phase answered the various self-tests in considerable detail. In contrast, students who submitted work late and showed evidence of inadequate research would similarly turn in self-tests with little sign of in-depth analysis.

Those preachers who have a genuine desire to communicate with clarity of thought will be the ones who take the time and make the effort to improve delivery. It will take hard work, but the importance of our task must motivate us to overcome the obstacle of inherent laziness, often masked by attention to the urgent rather than the necessary.

THE OBSTACLE OF RESISTANCE TO CHANGE

As a group, students tend to be quite open to change, since they are in training and are being graded partly for their willingness to conform to the set standards of their teacher. The results of the self-tests showed on the part of some a willingness to change beyond that of the classroom norm. Responses to the self-test on facial expression, for example, included the following comments: "My eyes do not always seem to express the same emotion as my face." "There are times when I seem unsure about how to express the words." "My facial expression was nondescript throughout the sermon." "I go through a very small range of facial expressions." After completing the self-tests, the students seemed much more anxious to undertake projects that would help them overcome specific weaknesses in their delivery.

Anyone who has been preaching for more than a few months may be surprised at the resistance to change that has subconsciously entered his or her approach to preaching. Take note, however, of the way you react to even incidental remarks people make about your sermons. One preacher told me about a man who would leave the auditorium almost every Sunday morning after tapping on his watch to remind the pastor that the sermon had gone overtime. That preacher had not taken the gesture as an incentive to evaluate his sermon length; he had taken it as a personal affront.

Most of us find it very difficult to accept criticisms of our sermons, either of their content or delivery. Even when I make an obvious error, like saying "Noah" when I mean "Jonah," I wish people would overlook it instead of calling it to my attention. That's human nature. But it is all the more reason why those who preach must learn to criticize themselves. We must learn to conduct a periodic and detailed self-examination in order to avoid the failures that inhibit communication. After all, most people will not criticize faulty delivery; they will just quit listening.

THE OBSTACLE OF EQUIPMENT

One variable that affected the quality of various self-tests in the case studies was equipment. Some individuals indicated that the playback equipment they used hindered them from completing all of the requirements of the self-tests. For example, several of the self-tests required the recording of location numbers on the videotape, but not all VCRs provided a read-out of such numbers. In other cases, the camera was not focused on the part of the body that the self-test analyzed. Some tests called for the camera to be set for a close-up to check the facial area; others, for a wide angle to show the entire torso. There is a temptation to attempt all the self-tests from the same camera angle, but that is impossible. The preacher must use the best possible equipment and use it as recommended by each self-test in order to profit from the exercises.

THE OBSTACLE OF THE INABILITY TO SELF-ANALYZE

The written responses to the self-tests indicated a wide variation in the ability of individuals to conduct self-analysis. The range of responses ran from single-word answers to detailed paragraphs about what individuals were observing on their own videotapes. Some were able to see details of facial and bodily movement that were totally overlooked by others.

The self-tests are diverse enough for preachers to use as extensively or intensively as they desire. Persons who have been preaching for any length of time should be better able to analyze themselves than those who are just starting out. Yet care should be taken not to allow familiarity to masquerade as effectiveness. We need to look at ourselves as if through the eyes of a stranger and see ourselves as others really see us. It may be difficult at first to submit to intensive self-analysis, but the reward of diligence will be a greater ability to express the message of God with confidence.

THE OBSTACLE OF INTOLERANCE OF AMBIGUITY

A book addressing the subject of sermon delivery includes some intentional ambiguity, since it is designed to function within a great variety of educational and experiential backgrounds. Some readers will find such ambiguity frustrating. They will desire more definite answers to potential problems rather than a range of answers that allow them to craft their own approach to preaching. This tendency became obvious when those in the case studies would add categories to some of the analysis devices or write in "maybe" in response to a "yes or no" question.

The purpose of this book is self-improvement. It is not designed to be a cookie-cutter that makes everyone who reads it sound like the author. It is not intended as a map to be followed but rather a territory to be explored. The exploration is just as important as the destination. But because this is the exploration of uncharted territory, it is more ambiguous than running a clearly marked cross-country trail. Don't let the obstacle of ambiguity deter you from your adventure.

This book will be of limited value to the casual reader. Its greatest value lies in the dedication of the individual preacher to time spent watching sermons and working on the self-tests. Corpses of sermons filed away in manila envelopes will not help the preacher prepare for future surgery. But carefully dissected sermons will prove invaluable in the development of greater skill in the pulpit. The reasons for not taking the time for self-analysis can be many, including job pressure, emotional stress, general fatigue, relationships, and the hundred and one activities of church life. However, the value of self-analysis in relation to sermon improvement cannot be overstated. Those who are willing to work through the self-tests in detail will recognize the value such personal analysis can produce. It will make you anxious to follow up the self-analysis with specific exercises for improvement.

Delivery must never be considered as an end but rather as a means to an end. Improvement of delivery skills must never be allowed to lull a person into the trap of inadequate preparation. Just because you can create interesting character voices does not eliminate the need for those characters to speak biblically. This approach to improving delivery has been carefully built on the philosophical foundation that content is of primary importance. What you say is always of greater value than how you say it.

Delivery, however, must not be relegated to a secular status when compared to the spiritual standing of exegetical research. Halford Luccock is right when he says, "Delivery has a soul as well as necessary mechanics."[2] All through the Old Testament emphasis was placed on the oral communication of God's message. "The word of the LORD came to me again, saying, 'Son of man, prophesy and say'" (Ezek. 30:1-2, NKJV). "And again the word of the LORD came to Haggai on the twenty-fourth day of the month, saying, 'Speak to Zerubbabel, governor of Judah, saying: "I will shake heaven and earth"'" (Hag. 2:20-21, NKJV). God's Word was usually an oral proclamation before it became a written Word. Now it is the task of our generation to take the written Word and effectively proclaim it once again as an oral proclamation.

The preacher of the Word of God must be totally dedicated to this task. Elements of personality, vocal faults, and unnatural body movements that hinder the proclamation of the message cannot be tolerated. Jay Adams reminds us, "If God's purpose is a joyful one, you dare not grind that through a personality grid that is so inflexible and insensitive that the message comes out drab or even solemn. In short, you must allow even your personality to be changed, if and when necessary, by God's truth."[3] If that is true of personality, it is also true of those qualities by which people identify your personality. Joy, sorrow, anger, peace, tranquility, fear, and sadness may be present in your heart, but they will never be communicated to an audience unless they are also present in your eyes, face, hands, tongue, and voice. We cannot effectively communicate the intent of God's Word unless our entire body becomes involved in the process. Adams continues, "The best preacher is the one who allows his voice and body to become a well-tuned instrument in the hands of the Holy Spirit."[4]

Any person who sets out to preach the Word of God has accepted a high calling. The message that has been given into our trust is beyond compare. God can convey through our preaching condemnation and judgment, on the one hand, and salvation and blessing on the other. We represent the Sovereign King of the universe as His heralds. Who is worthy of such a task? Yet who, choosing to undertake such a task, would not want to improve daily in the ability to do it? As the preacher's life is dedicated to the study and understanding of the Word, so may the preacher's body be dedicated to the effective delivery and communication of that Word.

Notes

Chapter 2

1. Jerry Vines, *A Guide to Effective Sermon Delivery* (Chicago: Moody Press, 1986), xiv.
2. Haddon Robinson, *Biblical Preaching* (Grand Rapids: Baker Book House, 1980), 191.
3. D. W. Cleverly Ford, *The Ministry of the Word* (Great Britain: Eerdmans, 1979), 222.
4. Henry J. Eggold, *Preaching Is Dialogue* (Grand Rapids: Baker Book House, 1980), 106.
5. Robinson, *Biblical Preaching*, 191-92.
6. Harold T. Bryson and James C. Taylor, *Building Sermons to Meet People's Needs* (Nashville: Broadman, 1980), 117.
7. John A. Broadus, *On the Preparation and Delivery of Sermons* (New York: Harper and Row, 1944), 8.
8. Robert Delnay, *Fire in Your Pulpit* (Schaumburg, Ill.: Regular Baptist Press, 1990), 79.
9. C. Jeff Woods, *User Friendly Evaluation* (New York: Alban Institute, 1995), 68.
10. Dwight E. Stevenson and Charles F. Diehl, *Reaching People from the Pulpit* (New York: Harper and Row, 1958), 3.
11. Richard Balge and Joel Gerlach, *Preach the Gospel* (Milwaukee: Northwestern Publishing, 1982), 111.
12. Ford, *Ministry of the Word*, 222.
13. David L. Larsen, *The Anatomy of Preaching* (Grand Rapids: Baker Book House, 1989), 182.
14. Woods, *User Friendly Evaluation*, 71.
15. Deane Kemper, *Effective Preaching* (Philadelphia: Westminster, 1985), 134.
16. Ford, *Ministry of the Word*, 222.
17. Walter Bowie, *Preaching* (New York: Abingdon Press, 1954), 212.
18. Art Fasol, *Essentials for Biblical Preaching* (Grand Rapids: Baker Book House, 1989), 115.
19. Stevenson and Diehl, *Reaching People from the Pulpit*, 13.
20. Lowell Erdahl, *Better Preaching* (St. Louis: Concordia, 1977), 7.
21. Donald Demaray, *An Introduction to Homiletics* (Grand Rapids: Baker, 1974), 122.
22. Stevenson and Diehl, *Reaching People from the Pulpit*, 2.

Chapter 3

1. Demaray, *Introduction to Homiletics*, 123.
2. Kemper, *Effective Preaching*, 135.
3. Erdahl, *Better Preaching*, 13.
4. James Berkley, *Preaching to Convince* (Waco, Tex.: Word, 1986), 82.
5. Thomas Chadwick, *Study of Non-Verbal Pulpit Communication* (Ann Arbor,

Mich.: Xerox University Microfilms, 1976), 26.

6. Kemper, *Effective Preaching*, 134.

7. Fasol, *Essentials for Biblical Preaching*, 130.

8. James Black, *The Mystery of Preaching* (Grand Rapids: Zondervan, 1978), 111.

9. Robert Burns, "To a Louse," *A Treasury of the Familiar* (New York: Rolier, 1942), 581.

10. Erdahl, *Better Preaching*, 6.

11. Black, *Mystery of Preaching*, 96.

Chapter 4

1. Halford E. Luccock, *In the Minister's Workshop* (New York: Abingdon, 1964), 182. Used by permission.

2. Lewis Carroll, *The Annotated Alice* (New York: Bramhall House, 1960), 270.

3. Jay Adams, *Pulpit Speech* (Grand Rapids: Baker Book House, 1972), 112.

4. Luccock, *In the Minister's Workshop*, 183-84. Used by permission.

5. W. E. Sangster, *Power in Preaching* (Grand Rapids: Baker Book House, 1958), 61.

6. Jay Adams, *Preaching with Purpose* (Grand Rapids: Zondervan, 1982), 105.

7. Paul S. Wilson, *The Practice of Preaching* (Nashville: Abingdon, 1995), 40.

8. Ibid.

9. Warren Wiersbe, *Preaching and Teaching with Imagination* (Grand Rapids: Baker Book House, 1996), 16-17.

10. *Congregations*, "Pastoral Wholeness: Preaching and Teaching That Heals" (November-December, 1993), 10.

11. Ibid., 12.

12. A. H. Strong, *Systematic Theology* (Valley Forge, Pa.: Judson, 1965), 718.

13. David Buttrick, *Homiletic: Moves and Structures* (Philadelphia: Fortress, 1987), 86.

14. Ibid., 94.

15. James B. Simpson, *Simpson's Contemporary Quotations* (Boston: Houghton Mifflin, 1988), 384.

16. Wiersbe, *Preaching and Teaching with Imagination*, 305.

17. Buttrick, *Homiletic*, 98.

Chapter 5

1. Roger Axtell, *Gestures* (New York: Wiley, 1991), 10.

2. Stevenson and Diehl, *Reaching People from the Pulpit*, 62.

3. Ibid., 64.

4. Lyle V. Mayer, *Fundamentals of Voice and Diction* (Dubuque, Iowa: William C. Brown, 1988), 31.

5. Ibid.

6. Axtell, *Gestures*, 69.

7. Ibid., 60.

8. John Hasling, *The Message, the Speaker, the Audience* (New York: McGraw Hill, 1982), 97.

9. Joseph DeVito, *Messages* (New York: Harper Collins, 1996), 146.

10. Richard Weaver, *Understanding Interpersonal Communications* (New York: Harper Collins, 1996), 221.

11. DeVito, *Messages*, 143.

12. Stevenson and Diehl, *Reaching People from the Pulpit*, 63.

13. Ibid.

14. Robert A. Allen, *Home Run to Heaven* (Milford, Mich.: Mott Media, 1985), 48-49. Used by permission.

Chapter 6

1. Kemper, *Effective Preaching*, 122.

2. Ian Pitt-Watson, *A Primer for Preachers* (Grand Rapids: Baker, 1986), 90.

3. Mayer, *Fundamentals of Voice and Diction*, 1.

4. Ibid., 2.

5. Virgil Anderson, *Training the Speaking Voice* (New York: Oxford University Press, 1977), 18.

6. Mayer, *Fundamentals of Voice and Diction*, 6.

7. Weaver, *Understanding Interpersonal Communication*, 227.

8. Anderson, *Training the Speaking Voice*, 31.

9. Stevenson and Diehl, *Reaching People from the Pulpit*, 41.

10. Mayer, *Fundamentals of Voice and Diction*, 24.

11. Robert Cohen, *Acting One* (Palo Alto, Calif.: Mayfield Publishing, 1984), 104.

12. Mayer, *Fundamentals of Voice and Diction*, 25.

13. Anderson, *Training the Speaking Voice*, 101.

14. Stevenson and Diehl, *Reaching People from the Pulpit*, 147-48.

15. Vines, *Guide to Effective Sermon Delivery*, 119.

16. J. Daniel Baumann, *An Introduction to Contemporary Preaching* (Grand Rapids: Baker, 1972), 192.

17. Larsen, *Anatomy of Preaching*, 182.

18. Cohen, *Acting One*, 122.

19. Ibid.

20. Warren Bennis and Brut Nanus, *Leaders* (New York: Harper and Row, 1985), 21.

21. John Piper, *The Supremacy of God in Preaching* (Grand Rapids: Baker, 1990), 101.

Chapter 7

1. Erdahl, *Better Preaching*, 15.

2. Luccock, *In the Minister's Workshop*, 193. Used by permission.

3. Adams, *Pulpit Speech*, 155.

4. Ibid.

Bibliography

Adams, Jay. *Preaching with Purpose.* Grand Rapids: Zondervan, 1982.
_____. *Pulpit Speech.* Grand Rapids: Baker Book House, 1972.
_____. *Sermon Analysis.* Denver: Accent Books, 1986.
Allen, Robert A. *Home Run to Heaven.* Milford, Mich.: Mott Media, 1985.
Allen, Ronald, and John Holbert. *Holy Root, Holy Branches.* Nashville: Abingdon Press, 1995.
Anderson, Virgil A. *Training the Speaking Voice.* New York: Oxford University Press, 1977.
Armstrong, Chloe. *Oral Interpretation of Biblical Literature.* Minneapolis: Burgess, 1968.
Axtell, Roger. *Gestures.* New York: Wiley, 1991.
Bacon, Wallace A. *The Art of Interpretation.* New York: Holt, Rinehart and Winston, 1979.
Balge, Richard, and Joel Gerlach. *Preach the Gospel.* Milwaukee: Northwestern Publishing House, 1982.
Baumann, J. Daniel. *An Introduction to Contemporary Preaching.* Grand Rapids: Baker Book House, 1972.
Barrett, Ethel. *Storytelling—It's Easy.* Grand Rapids: Zondervan, 1960.
Barton, Robert. *Acting Onstage and Off.* New York: Holt, Rinehart and Winston, Inc., 1989.
Bennis, Warren, and Burt Nanus. *Leaders.* New York: Harper and Row, 1985.
Berkley, James D., ed. *Preaching to Convince.* Waco, Tex.: Word, 1986.
Black, James. *The Mystery of Preaching.* Grand Rapids: Zondervan, 1978.
Blackwood, Andrew. *Expository Preaching for Today.* Nashville: Abingdon-Cokesbury, 1953.
Bodey, Richard A. *If I Had Only One Sermon to Preach.* Grand Rapids: Baker, 1994.
Bowie, Walter Russell. *Preaching.* New York: Abingdon Press, 1954.
Braga, James. *How to Prepare Bible Messages.* Portland, Oreg.: Multnomah, 1969.
Broadus, John A. *On the Preparation and Delivery of Sermons.* New York: Harper and Row, 1944.
Brown, Steve, Haddon Robinson, and William Willimon. *A Voice in the Wilderness.* Sisters, Oreg.: Multnomah Press, 1993.
Bryson, Harold T., and James C. Taylor. *Building Sermons to Meet People's Needs.* Nashville: Broadman, 1980.
Buttrick, David. *Homiletic: Moves and Structures.* Philadelphia: Fortress, 1987.

Carroll, Lewis. *The Annotated Alice*. New York: Bramhall House, 1960.

Carson, D. A., and John D. Woodbridge. *God and Culture*. Grand Rapids: Eerdmans, 1993.

Chadwick, Thomas. *Study of Non-Verbal Pulpit Communication*. Ann Arbor, Mich.: Xerox University Microfilms, 1976.

Childers, Jana. *Performing the Word*. Nashville: Abingdon, 1998.

Cohen, Robert. *Acting One*. Palo Alto, Calif.: Mayfield Publishing, 1984.

Dabney, Robert L. *Sacred Rhetoric*. Carlisle, Pa.: Banner of Truth, 1979.

Delnay, Robert G. *Fire in Your Pulpit*. Schaumburg, Ill.: Regular Baptist Press, 1990.

Demaray, Donald E. *An Introduction to Homiletics*. Grand Rapids: Baker Book House, 1974.

DeVito, Joseph A. *Messages*. New York: HarperCollins, 1996.

Eggold, Henry J. *Preaching Is Dialogue*. Grand Rapids: Baker Book House, 1980.

Ellingsen, Mark. *The Integrity of Biblical Narrative*. Minneapolis: Fortress, 1990.

Erdahl, Lowell. *Better Preaching*. St. Louis: Concordia, 1977.

Fasol, Al. *Essentials for Biblical Preaching*. Grand Rapids: Baker, 1989.

Faucette, Joey. "Pastoral Wholeness: Preaching and Teaching That Heals," *Congregations* (November-December 1993): 10-14.

Felleman, Hazel. *The Best Loved Poems of the American People*. New York: Garden City Publishing, 1936.

Ford, D. W. Cleverly. *The Ministry of the Word*. Great Britain: Eerdmans, 1979.

Gillensen, Lewis W. *Billy Graham and Seven Who Were Saved*. New York: Pocket Books, 1967.

Gunther, Peter F. *Great Sermons of the 20th Century*. Westchester, Ill.: Crossway Books, 1986.

Hall, E. Eugene, and James L. Heflin. *Proclaim the Word*. Nashville: Broadman Press, 1985.

Hasling, John. *The Message, the Speaker, the Audience*. New York: McGraw Hill, 1982.

Holbert, John. *Preaching Old Testament*. Nashville: Abingdon Press, 1991.

Jones, Bob. *How to Improve Your Preaching*. New York: Fleming H. Revell, 1945.

Kaiser, Walter, "The Crisis in Expository Preaching Today," *Preaching* (September-October 1995).

Kemper, Deane A. *Effective Preaching*. Philadelphia: Westminster Press, 1985.

Ketcham, Donn. *No Uncertain Sound*. Cherry Hill, N.J.: Association of Baptists for World Evangelism, 1982.

Kroll, Woodrow M. *Prescription for Preaching*. Grand Rapids: Baker Book House, 1980.

Larsen, David L. *The Anatomy of Preaching.* Grand Rapids: Baker Book House, 1989.

Lee, Charlotte I., and Timothy Gura. *Oral Interpretation.* Boston: Houghton Mifflin, 1992.

Lee, Jung Young. *Korean Preaching.* Nashville: Abingdon, 1997.

Lewis, Todd. *Communicating Literature.* Dubuque, Iowa: Kendall/Hunt Publishing Company, 1991.

Lewis, Ralph L. and Gregg. *Inductive Preaching.* Westchester, Ill.: Crossway Books, 1983.

Lewis, Ralph L. and Gregg. *Learning to Preach like Jesus.* Westchester, Ill.: Crossway Books, 1989.

Liefeld, Walter. *New Testament Exposition.* Grand Rapids: Zondervan, 1984.

Lishcher, Richard. *Theories of Preaching: Selected Readings in the Homiletical Tradition.* Durham, N.C.: Labyrinth Press, 1987.

Long, Thomas G. *The Witness of Preaching.* Louisville, Ky.: Westminster, 1989.

Luccock, Halford E. *In the Minister's Workshop.* New York: Abingdon, 1964.

Massey, James Earl. *The Sermon in Perspective.* Grand Rapids: Baker Book House, 1976.

Matheny, Tim. *Reaching the Arabs.* Pasadena, Calif.: William Carey Library, 1981.

Mayer, Lyle V. *Fundamentals of Voice and Diction.* Dubuque, Iowa: William C. Brown, 1988.

Miller, Calvin. *Spirit, Word and Story.* Grand Rapids: Baker, 1996.

Nichols, J. Randall. *Building the Word.* New York: Harper and Row, 1980.

Olmstead, Robert. *Elements of the Writing Craft.* Cincinnati: Story Press, 1997.

Parrott, Leslie. *Building Today's Church.* Grand Rapids: Baker Book House, 1973.

Philibert, Michel. *Christ's Preaching and Ours.* Richmond, Va.: John Knox, 1964.

Philpot, William M. *Best Black Sermons.* Valley Forge, Pa.: Judson, 1972.

Piper, John. *The Supremacy of God in Preaching.* Grand Rapids: Baker, 1990.

Pitt-Watson, Ian. *A Primer for Preachers.* Grand Rapids: Baker, 1986.

Reu, M. *Homiletics.* Grand Rapids: Baker Book House, 1967.

Riley, W. B. *The Preacher and His Preaching.* Wheaton, Ill.: Sword of the Lord Publishers, 1948.

Robinson, Haddon. *Biblical Preaching.* Grand Rapids: Baker Book House, 1980.

Roloff, Leland. *The Perception and Evocation of Literature.* Glenview, Ill.: Scott Foresman, 1973.

Sangster, W. E. *Power in Preaching.* Grand Rapids: Baker Book House, 1958.

Seamands, John T. *Tell It Well.* Kansas City: Beacon Hill Press of Kansas City, 1981.

Simpson, James B. *Simpson's Contemporary Quotations.* Boston: Houghton Mifflin, 1988.

Spurgeon, Charles. *Lectures to My Students.* Grand Rapids: Zondervan, 1965.

Stevenson, Dwight E., and Charles F. Diehl. *Reaching People from the Pulpit.* New York: Harper and Row, 1958.

Stott, John R. W. *Between Two Worlds: The Art of Preaching in the Twentieth Century.* Grand Rapids: Eerdmans, 1982.

Strong, A. H. *Systematic Theology.* Valley Forge, Pa.: Judson Press, 1965.

Swank, George W. *Dialogic Style in Preaching.* Valley Forge, Pa.: Judson Press, 1981.

Thomas, Gary. "The Return of the Jewish Church," *Christianity Today* (September 7, 1998).

Trenholm, Sarah, and Arthur Jensen. *Interpersonal Communication.* Belmont, Calif.: Wadsworth, 1992.

Vines, Jerry. *A Guide to Effective Sermon Delivery.* Chicago: Moody Press, 1986.

Weaver, Richard L. *Understanding Interpersonal Communication.* New York: HarperCollins, 1996.

Wiersbe, Warren W. *Preaching and Teaching with Imagination.* Grand Rapids: Baker Book House, 1996.

Wilson, Paul S. *The Practice of Preaching.* Nashville: Abingdon, 1995.

Woods, C. Jeff. *User Friendly Evaluation.* New York: Alban Institute, 1995.

Yordon, Judy. *Roles in Interpretation.* Dubuque, Iowa: William C. Brown Publishers, 1989.